PRENTICE HALL

ALGEBRA
TOOLS FOR A CHANGING WORLD

Chapter 8
Support File

Exponents and
Exponential Functions

PRENTICE HALL
Upper Saddle River, New Jersey
Needham Heights, Massachusetts

ISBN: 0-13-433332-2

Printed in the United States of America
1 2 3 4 5 6 7 8   02 01 00 99 98 97

Editorial, design, and production services: Publishers Resource Group, Inc.

PRENTICE HALL
Simon & Schuster Education Group
A VIACOM COMPANY

Chapter 8

Exponents and Exponential Functions

Alternative Activity: Teacher's Notes **for 8-2A**

Exponential Growth

TYPE OF ACTIVITY: Technology (Graphing calculator)

CONCEPTS: This Alternative Activity covers the same concepts as the Work Together on page 367 in the student text. Students use the graphing calculator to explore an exponential function.

MATERIALS: Graphing calculator; Alternative Activity 8-2A student worksheet

---

FACILITATING THE ACTIVITY

For this activity, students work with a partner. One person can act as the recorder and the other can work with the graphing calculator. Both should agree on an answer before writing it down.

The directions used in this lesson are for the TI-82. Detailed instructions on how to perform various operations for several different calculators are given in the Graphing Calculator Handbook.

Exercise 1

After students have written the equation and identified it as a linear equation, ask: *What is the y-intercept?* **(0, 4.9)** *What is the slope of the line?* **0.8**

Exercise 2

To enter the equation, students use the ▮**Y=**▮ key. Range values for the variables can be changed using ▮WINDOW▮. Students should realize that only quadrant I is appropriate for this graph. Ask: *What should be the value for Xmin?* **0** *What should be the value for Xmax?* **5** Let students explore *y*-value ranges until their graph shows *y*-values for all *x*-values between 0 and 5. The values Ymin = 0 and Ymax = 10 will work well.

Before introducing the exponential function for Job B, make sure students understand that a 5% increase in an amount means you have 105% of the original amount. To find 105%, multiply by 1.05.

Exercise 3

Students press ▮**Y=**▮ and enter the exponential equation as Y_2. The correct keystrokes are
6 ▮×▮ 1.05 ▮∧▮ ▮X,T,θ▮ .

Exercise 4

Students should realize that in order to answer this question, it is necessary to find the year in which Job B starts to pay less than Job A. The best way to do this is to use [TABLE]. Students should see that for $x < 3$, the value of Y_1 is greater than the value of Y_2. For $x \geq 3$, the value of Y_2 is greater than the value of Y_1.

In this activity, students compare the two jobs over a five-year period. After they have completed the activity, ask: *Do you think Job A would remain higher paying than Job B forever?* Have students use ▮WINDOW▮ to change the variable ranges.

Xmin=0	Xmax=50	Xscl=1
Ymin=0	Ymax=100	Yscl=1

Ask: *Do the functions cross a second time?* **yes** Have them use [TABLE] to discover that after 35 years Job B would become the higher-paying job again. Ask: *Do you think the graphs will cross again?* **no** If students are not convinced by the shape of the graphs, they can extend the ranges again.

Alternative Activity: Student Worksheet **for 8-2A**

Exponential Growth

Work with a partner.

Suppose you are offered a choice of two jobs. Job A has a starting wage of $4.90/h, with an $.80 raise every year. Job B starts at $6.00/h with a 5% raise every year.

> **What You'll Learn**
> Using the graphing calculator to explore exponential growth
>
> **What You'll Need**
> Graphing calculator

1. Let $x = $ the number of years on the job and $y = $ the hourly wage. Write an equation to show how the wages for Job A grow. What kind of function does your equation represent?

2. Graph the function using the graphing calculator. With your partner, decide what ranges you should use for the variables. Your graph should show the wages from the start of the job through the fifth-year raise.

You can use an exponential function to show how the wages for Job B grow.

beginning wage

new wage $\longrightarrow$ $y = 6 \cdot 1.05^x$ $\longleftarrow$ **number of wage increases**

105% as a decimal

Because multiplying over and over by 1.05 causes the wage to increase, this kind of exponential function is an example of *exponential growth*.

3. Graph the function for Job B on the same set of axes as the function for Job A. Press [Y=] [▼] to enter the exponential equation as **Y2**.

4. Based on the wage, when would you prefer to have Job A or Job B? Explain.

Alternative Activity: Teacher's Notes **for 8-2B**

Exponential Growth

TYPE OF ACTIVITY: Technology (Spreadsheet software)

CONCEPTS: This Alternative Activity covers the same concepts as Example 2 on page 369 in the student text. Students use spreadsheet software to solve problems involving compound interest.

MATERIALS: Calculator; Spreadsheet software; Alternative Activity 8-2B student worksheet

---

FACILITATING THE ACTIVITY

Before beginning the activity, review the definitions of principal and interest. *Principal* is the amount of money you put in a bank account. *Interest* is the amount the bank pays you for letting them use your money.

The directions used in this lesson are for the TI-82. Detailed instructions on how to perform various operations for several different calculators are given in the Graphing Calculator Handbook.

Exercise 1

To use a calculator to evaluate the exponential function, press **200** ⊠ **1.07** ⏶ **5** [ENTER] or **200** ⊠ **1.07** $\boxed{y^x}$ **5** ▤.

Remind students to round their answer to the nearest cent.

Spreadsheet programs may differ slightly. The directions given in this lesson are for *Microsoft Excel*. If you are using a different spreadsheet program, refer to your program handbook.

Exercise 3

If you are using Microsoft Excel, the formula is =A2*B2^C2.

ERROR ALERT! Some students using *Microsoft Excel* may omit the = sign when writing a formula. **Remediation:** Point out that *Microsoft Excel* will not evaluate the formula if the = sign is omitted.

Exercises 4-6

Students must press [RETURN] after they enter each new value for *a*, *b*, and *x*.

Exercise 6

Students can solve this problem using Guess and Test. After 14 years the balance will be $1468.60. After 15 years the balance will be $1586.08.

Some students may want to further explore the use of the spreadsheet. As an alternative to changing the values of *a*, *b*, and *x* for each new problem, they could extend the spreadsheet so that they can use a new row for each new problem. By using the **Copy** command, they will not need to key in the formula for *y* in each row.

Move the cursor to cell D2. Select **Copy** from the **Edit** menu. Highlight cells D3 through D24. Select **Paste** from the **Edit** menu. Then press [ESC] and move the cursor to A3 and begin to enter values for *a*, *b*, and *x*. Notice that the formula is copied in such a way that it applies to the data entered in the same row.

When students have completed the activity, encourage them to make up other compound interest problems to solve.

Students can save this spreadsheet to use at another time. To do this, select **Save As** from the **File** menu. Type in a new name for the spreadsheet and save.

Alternative Activity: Student Worksheet **for 8-2B**

Exponential Growth

When a bank pays interest on both the principal and the interest an account has already earned, the bank is paying **compound interest**. An **interest period** is the length of time over which interest is calculated. Compound interest is an exponential situation.

> **What You'll Learn**
> Using spreadsheet software to solve problems involving compound interest
>
> **What You'll Need**
> Calculator; Spreadsheet software

Example

You deposit $200 in an account paying 7% interest, compounded annually. Find the account balance after five years.

You can use an exponential function of the form $y = ab^x$.

initial deposit
↓
balance in account ⟶ $y = 200 \cdot 1.07^5$ ⟵ **number of interest payments**
↑
107% as a decimal

1. Use a calculator to find the account balance.

You can use spreadsheet software to create a spreadsheet that will enable you to calculate the balance quickly.

2. In cells A1, B1, C1, and D1, enter the variable names a, b, x, y. These will serve as the labels for the columns in the spreadsheet.

3. Enter the value of a (from the problem above) in cell A2. Enter the value of b in cell B2 and the value of x in cell C2.

4. In cell D2, enter a formula for ab^x using A2, B2, and C2 for a, b, and x respectively. When you have finished entering the formula, press [RETURN]. The number 280.51034 should appear in cell D2. To format this as currency, move the cursor back to cell D2. Select **Format Cells** from the menu. Then select currency as the format for cell D2. $280.51 will appear in the cell.

Change the values of a, b, and x to solve each problem.

5. What would be the amount in the account after ten years?

6. If the interest rate were 8%, what would be the amount in the account after ten years?

7. How many years would it take $500 to triple at 8% interest?

Alternate Activity: Teacher's Notes **for 8-4**

Zero and Negative Exponents

TYPE OF ACTIVITY: Technology (Calculator)

CONCEPTS: This Alternative Activity covers the same concepts as Example 2 on page 380 in the student text. Students use the calculator to discover the definition of a negative exponent.

MATERIALS: Calculator; Alternative Activity 8-4 student worksheet

---

FACILITATING THE ACTIVITY

Students should work with a partner for this activity. Students will be collecting data, looking for patterns, and making generalizations in order to discover the definition of a negative exponent. Working with a partner on tasks such as these will be important to students' learning to work together cooperatively. For example, scientists often work together to make discoveries in a laboratory.

The directions used in this lesson are for the TI-82. Detailed instructions on how to perform various operations for several different calculators are given in the Graphing Calculator Handbook.

Exercise 1

To evaluate 2^1 on a calculator, press **2** $\boxed{\wedge}$ **1** $\boxed{\text{ENTER}}$.

Exercises 5–8

In many exercises involving fractions, students must place parentheses around the complete numerator and/or denominator. These exercises do not require parentheses since there are no operation signs in either the numerator or denominator.

Exercises 9–12

Students will get a syntax error if they use the $\boxed{-}$ key rather than the $\boxed{(-)}$ key.

ERROR ALERT! Some students may assume that 2^{-1} is the same as -2. **Remediation:** Students need practice with activities such as this one to be convinced of the definition of a negative exponent. Be sure they use their calculators before they write down a value.

Exercises 14–17

Before students begin, ask:

- *What is 10^1?* **10**
- *What is 10^2?* **100**
- *What is 10^3?* **1000**
- *What is 10^4?* **10,000**
- *What is the decimal equivalent of $\frac{1}{10}$?* **0.1**
- *What is the decimal equivalent of $\frac{1}{100}$?* **0.01**
- *What is the decimal equivalent of $\frac{1}{1000}$?* **0.001**
- *What is the decimal equivalent of $\frac{1}{10,000}$?* **0.0001**

Exercises 18–21

ERROR ALERT! Students may omit the parentheses when entering the expression. **Remediation:** Point out that it is -2, not 2, which is being raised to the power.

Exercises 22–25

ERROR ALERT! Students may use parentheses when entering the expression. **Remediation:** Point out that it is 10, not -10, which is being raised to the power.

Exercise 26

Ask: *Why can't zero be raised to a negative exponent?* **Division by zero is undefined**.

Alternative Activity Student Worksheet **for 8-4**

• •

Zero and Negative Exponents

Use a calculator to evaluate each expression.

1. 2^1	**2.** 2^2	**3.** 2^3	**4.** 2^4
5. $\frac{1}{2^1}$	**6.** $\frac{1}{2^2}$	**7.** $\frac{1}{2^3}$	**8.** $\frac{1}{2^4}$
9. 2^{-1}	**10.** 2^{-2}	**11.** 2^{-3}	**12.** 2^{-4}

> **What You'll Learn**
> Using a calculator to discover the formula for negative exponents
>
> **What You'll Need**
> Calculator

13. Look at the pattern in each column of exercises above. Use the pattern to write an expression for 2^{-5} that uses a positive exponent.

Predict the decimal equivalent for each expression and check your prediction with the calculator. Then write the expression as a fraction with a positive exponent.

14. 10^{-1}	**15.** 10^{-2}	**16.** 10^{-3}	**17.** 10^{-4}
18. $(-2)^{-1}$	**19.** $(-2)^{-2}$	**20.** $(-2)^{-3}$	**21.** $(-2)^{-4}$
22. -10^{-1}	**23.** -10^{-2}	**24.** -10^{-3}	**25.** -10^{-4}

26. Complete the following definition of a negative exponent.
For any nonzero number a, $a^{-n} = $?

You can use what you know about rewriting the expression a^{-n} to see how the values of a^n and a^{-n} are related.

$$a^n \cdot a^{-n} = a^n \cdot \frac{1}{a^n}$$
$$= \frac{a^n}{1} \cdot \frac{1}{a^n}$$
$$= 1$$

Therefore a^n and a^{-n} are *reciprocals*.

Use the calculator to evaluate each product and verify that a^n and a^{-n} are reciprocals.

27. $4^2 \cdot 4^{-2}$ **28.** $3^4 \cdot 3^{-4}$ **29.** $5^3 \cdot 5^{-3}$

Reteaching 8-1

∙∙

OBJECTIVE: Examining patterns in exponential functions	**MATERIALS:** None

To write an exponential pattern as a function with a variable, follow these steps:

   1. Make a table of the data.

   2. Find the pattern.

   3. Write an equation with exponents.

Example

You have ten CDs. That number doubles every year. How many CDs will you have at the end of 5 yr?

Step 1 Make a table.

Time	No. of CDs
0	10
1 yr	$10 \cdot 2$
2 yrs	$10 \cdot 2 \cdot 2$
3 yrs	$10 \cdot 2 \cdot 2 \cdot 2$

Step 2 Find the pattern.

$10 \cdot 2 \longrightarrow$ After 1 yr

$10 \cdot 2^2 \longrightarrow$ After 2 yr

$10 \cdot 2^3 \longrightarrow$ After 3 yr

$10 \cdot 2^n \longrightarrow$ After n yr

Step 3 Write an equation with exponents and solve.

$c = 10 \cdot 2^n \longleftarrow$ **Write the equation.**

$c = 10 \cdot 2^5 \longleftarrow$ **Substitute 5 for n.**

$c = 320 \longleftarrow$ **Use a calculator.**

You will have 320 CDs at the end of 5 yr.

Activity

Follow the above steps to write and evaluate the function.

   1. Your science class is collecting cans. You start with 150 cans. Your collection triples every week. How many cans will you have collected after 7 wk?

   2. A population of 2500 triples in size every 10 yr. What will the population be in 30 yr?

   3. Your parents invested $2000 in a college fund for you when you were 4 yr old. It has doubled in value every 4 yr. If you are now 16, how much is in your college fund?

   4. A bacteria culture doubles in size every 8 h. The culture starts with 150 cells. How many will there be after 24 h? After 72 h?

Reteaching 8-2

OBJECTIVE: Modeling exponential growth	MATERIALS: None

To write an exponential function to find growth, follow these steps.

Step 1 Find the initial amount a.

Step 2 Multiply by the growth factor b, which occurs over x time periods.

Step 3 After the x time periods, the new amount will be $a \times b^x$.

The function is written $y = a \cdot b^x$.

Example

The cost of a car is $10,000. Suppose the price increases 5% each year. What will the cost be at the end of 10 yr? What if the price increases 7% each year? Use the table below to find the amounts.

a (initial amount)	b (growth factor)	x (number of increases)	y (new amount)
10,000	$100\% + 5\% = 105\%$ $= 1.05$	10	$10{,}000 \cdot 1.05^{10} = y$
10,000	$100\% + 7\% = 107\%$ $= 1.07$	10	$10{,}000 \cdot 1.07^{10} = y$

The cost at the end of 10 yr with a growth factor of 5% will be $16,289; at 7% it will be $19,672.

Activity

Write an exponential function to model each situation. Find each amount at the end of the specified time. Round your answers to the nearest whole number.

1. A town with a population of 5,000 grows 3% per year. Find the population at the end of 10 yr.

2. The price of a bicycle is $100. It increases 8% per year. What will the price be at the end of 5 yr?

3. A 2 ft-tall tree grows 10% per year. How tall will the tree be at the end of 8 yr?

Reteaching 8-3

•••

OBJECTIVE: Modeling exponential decay	**MATERIALS:** None

To write an exponential function to find decay, you must use the initial amount a and the decay factor b. With decay b, the base is between 0 and 1. For $0 < b < 1$, the function $y = a \cdot b^x$ can be used to model decay.

Example

In 1991, the average American diet consisted of 35.5% fat. There has been a decrease of 2.5% every year. Find the percent of fat in the average American's diet 5 yr later.

$100\% - 2.5\% = 97.5\%$ ⟵ **Subtract the percent of decrease from 100% to find the decay factor.**

$97.5\% = 0.975$ ⟵ **Convert the decay factor to a decimal.**

$y = 35.5 \cdot 0.975^x$ ⟵ **Write the function where y represents the amount of fat and x represents the number of years since 1986.**

$y = 35.5 \cdot 0.975^5$ ⟵ **Use 5 for x because this represents the number of years.**

$y = 31.3$ ⟵ **Use a calculator.**

The percent of fat in the average American's diet in 5 yr is 31.3%.

Activity

Identify the decay factor in each function.

1. $y = 10 \cdot 0.4^x$ **2.** $f(x) = 5 \cdot 0.2^x$ **3.** $g(x) = 100 \cdot \left(\frac{4}{5}\right)^x$

Write an exponential function to model each situation. Find the amount at the end of the specified time.

4. $1,000 purchase
10% loss in value each year
5 yr

5. $5,000 investment
13.5% loss each year
8 yr

6. 20,000 population
12.5% annual decrease
10 yr

Reteaching 8-4

· ·

OBJECTIVE: Evaluating and simplifying expressions in which zero and negative numbers are used as exponents	**MATERIALS:** None

- When a nonzero number a has a zero exponent, then $a^0 = 1$.
- For any nonzero number a and any integer n, $a^n = \dfrac{1}{a^n}$.

Example

Write 5^{-2} as a simple fraction.

5^{-2}

$\dfrac{5^{-2}}{1}$ ⟵   **Rewrite as a fraction when necessary.**

$\dfrac{1}{5^2}$ ⟵   **Since *negative* means *opposite*, move any expression that contains a negative exponent to the opposite side of the fraction bar.**

$\dfrac{1}{5^2}$ ⟵   **If the entire numerator moves to the denominator, a 1 must be written in the numerator.**

$\dfrac{1}{25}$ ⟵   **Simplify.**

Activity

Write each expression as an integer, a simple fraction, or an expression that contains only positive exponents.

1. 10^{-3}

2. 1.67^0

3. 5^{-4}

4. 7^{-3}

5. $\left(\dfrac{-3}{2}\right)^{-2}$

6. $(5x)^{-4}$

7. 4^{-1}

8. 376.5^0

9. b^{-5}

Additional Exercises

Write each expression so that it contains only positive exponents.

10. $\left(\dfrac{2}{7}\right)^{-4}$

11. $3ab^0$

12. -4^{-3}

13. $a^{-3}b^{-4}$

14. $\dfrac{3x^{-2}}{y}$

15. $12xy^{-3}$

16. $\dfrac{8}{4^{-2}}$

17. $\dfrac{(3x)^{-1}}{4}$

· ·

Reteaching 8-5

•••

OBJECTIVE: Writing numbers in scientific notation   **MATERIALS:** None

To write a number in **scientific notation**, follow these steps:

- Move the decimal to the right of the first integer.

- Multiply by 10^n, where n represents the number of places the decimal was moved.

- A positive exponent indicates a large number. A negative exponent indicates a small number, usually with many decimal places.

Examples

Write 9,040,000,000 and 0.000 000 8 in scientific notation.

9,040,000,000	⟵ **standard form**
9.040 000 000.	⟵ **Move the decimal to the left 9 places.**
9.04×10^9	⟵ **Drop all insignificant 0's. Multiply by the appropriate power of 10.**
0.000 000 8	⟵ **standard form**
0.000 000 8.	⟵ **Move the decimal to the right 7 places.**
8.0×10^{-7}	⟵ **Multiply by the appropriate power of 10.**

Activity

Write each number in scientific notation.

1. 420,000   **2.** 5,100,000,000   **3.** 260 billion

4. 830 million   **5.** 0.00075   **6.** 0.004005

Additional Exercises

Write each number in standard notation.

7. 6.345×10^8 **8.** 3.2×10^{-5} **9.** 4.081×10^6 **10.** 2.581×10^{-3}

Reteaching 8-6

· ·

OBJECTIVE: Multiplying powers with the same bases

MATERIALS: None

- A power is an expression in the form a^n.

- To multiply powers with the same base, add the exponents.

  $a^m \cdot a^n = a^{m+n}$

Example

Simplify $4^6 \cdot 4^3$.

$$4^6 \cdot 4^3$$
$$= 4^{6+3} \qquad \longleftarrow \textbf{Rewrite as one base with the exponents added.}$$
$$= 4^9 \qquad \longleftarrow \textbf{Add the exponents.}$$

So $4^6 \cdot 4^3 = 4^9$.

Activity

Complete each equation.

1. $8^2 \cdot 8^3 = 8^{\blacksquare}$

2. $2^{\blacksquare} \cdot 2^6 = 2^9$

3. $a^{12} \cdot a^{\blacksquare} = a^{15}$

4. $x^{\blacksquare} \cdot x^5 = x^6$

5. $b^{-4} \cdot b^3 = b^{\blacksquare}$

6. $6^4 \cdot 6^{\blacksquare} = 6^2$

7. $3^4 \cdot 3^8 = 3^{\blacksquare}$

8. $c^{\blacksquare} \cdot c^{-7} = c^{11}$

9. $10^{-6} \cdot 10^{-3} = 10^{\blacksquare}$

Additional Exercises

Simplify each expression.

10. $3x^2 \cdot 4x \cdot 2x^3$

11. $m^2 \cdot 3m^4 \cdot 6a \cdot a^{-3}$

12. $p^3 q^{-1} \cdot p^2 q^{-8}$

· ·

Algebra Chapter 8   A Multiplication Property of Exponents   **15**

Reteaching 8-7

· ·

OBJECTIVE: Using two more multiplication properties of exponents

MATERIALS: None

- To raise a power to a power, think of it as power *of* a power. Since *of* means to multiply, you multiply the exponents together.

- Every number and variable inside parentheses is being raised to the power to the right of the parentheses.

Example

Simplify $(4x^3)^2$.

$(4x^3)^2$

$(4^1x^3)^2$ ⟵ **Rewrite each number and variable with an exponent.**

$(4^1x^3)^2$ ⟵ **Draw arrows from the exponent outside the parentheses to each exponent inside the parentheses.**

$4^{2\cdot1}x^{2\cdot3}$ ⟵ **Rewrite showing the exponents to be multiplied.**

4^2x^6 ⟵ **Multiply the exponents.**

$16x^6$ ⟵ **Simplify.**

Activity

Draw arrows from the exponent outside the parentheses to each exponent inside the parentheses. Then simplify each expression.

1. $(5^2)^4$ **2.** $(a^5)^4$ **3.** $(2^3)^2$ **4.** $(4x)^3$

5. $(7a^4)^2$ **6.** $(3g^2)^3$ **7.** $(g^2h^3)^5$ **8.** $(s^6)^2$

Additional Exercises

Simplify each expression.

9. $(x^2y^4)^3$ **10.** $(3r^5)^0$ **11.** $g^9 \cdot g^{-7}$

12. $(c^4)^7$ **13.** $(3.2)^5 \cdot (3.2)^{-5}$ **14.** $(8ab^6)^3$

Reteaching 8-8

• •

OBJECTIVE: Applying division properties of exponents	**MATERIALS:** None

To divide powers with the same base, subtract exponents.

Example

Simplify $\frac{4^3}{4^5}$.

$$\frac{4^3}{4^5}$$

$\frac{4 \cdot 4 \cdot 4}{4 \cdot 4 \cdot 4 \cdot 4 \cdot 4}$ ⟵   **Expand the numerator and the denominator.**

$\frac{\cancel{4} \cdot \cancel{4} \cdot \cancel{4}}{\cancel{4} \cdot \cancel{4} \cdot \cancel{4} \cdot 4 \cdot 4}$ ⟵   **Draw lines through terms that are in both the numerator and the denominator.**

$\frac{1}{4 \cdot 4}$ ⟵   **Cancel.**

$\frac{1}{4^2}$ or 4^{-2} ⟵   **Rewrite with exponents.**

$3 - 5 = -2$ ⟵   **Subtract the exponents from the original equation. Compare this to the exponent in the first answer.**

So $\frac{4^3}{4^5} = 4^{3-5} = 4^{-2}$.

$\frac{1}{4^2}$ ⟵   **Write with positive exponents.**

To raise a quotient to a power use repeated multiplication.

Activity

Use both methods shown in the Example to simplify each expression. Use only positive exponents.

1. $\frac{z^6}{z^3}$ **2.** $\left(\frac{3^2}{4}\right)^3$ **3.** $\frac{m^{-3}}{m^{-4}}$ **4.** $\left(\frac{5^3}{5^4}\right)$ **5.** $\left(\frac{b^7}{b^5}\right)^3$

6. $\frac{5a^5}{15a^2}$ **7.** $\frac{2^2}{2^5}$ **8.** $\frac{d^8}{d^3}$ **9.** $\frac{x^7}{x^5}$ **10.** $\left(\frac{10^8}{10^2}\right)^3$

Practice 8-1
• •
Example Exercises

Example 1

Complete the table for each exercise.

1. The number of cells doubles every hour.

Time	Number of Cells
Initial	100
1 h	200
2 h	400
3 h	■
4 h	■
5 h	■
6 h	■

2. The investment doubles every 8 yr.

Time	Investment Worth
Initial	$500
8 yr	$1000
16 yr	$2000
24 yr	$4000
32 yr	■
■	■
■	■

3. The number of insects triples every 2 mo.

Time	Number of Insects
Initial	20
2 mo	60
4 mo	180
6 mo	■
8 mo	■
■	■
■	■

Example 2

Evaluate each exponential function.

4. $y = 3^x$ for $x = 1, 2,$ and 4

5. $y = 2^x$ for $x = 2, 3,$ and 5

6. $y = 2.5^x$ for $x = 2, 3,$ and 4

7. $y = 0.3^x$ for $x = 1, 4,$ and 5

8. $y = 100 \cdot 2^x$ for $x = 4, 5,$ and 6

9. $y = 200 \cdot 0.5^x$ for $x = 1, 3,$ and 4

10. $y = 2000 \cdot 3^x$ for $x = 3$ and 5

11. $y = 25 \cdot 5^x$ for $x = 1, 3,$ and 4

12. $y = \left(\frac{1}{3}\right)^x$ for $x = 1, 2,$ and 4

13. $y = \left(\frac{2}{5}\right)^x$ for $x = 1, 2,$ and 3

14. $y = 4096\left(\frac{1}{2}\right)^x$ for $x = 3$

15. $y = 125\left(\frac{4}{5}\right)^x$ for $x = 2, 3,$ and 4

Example 3

Graph each function.

16. $y = 4^x$

17. $y = 8^x$

18. $y = 2.5^x$

19. $y = 5^x$

20. $y = 4 \cdot 1.5^x$

21. $y = 4 \cdot 2^x$

22. $y = \frac{1}{5} \cdot 5^x$

23. $y = \frac{1}{9} \cdot 3^x$

24. $y = 8\left(\frac{1}{2}\right)^x$

Practice 8-1

•••

Mixed Exercises

Complete the table for each exercise.

1. Investment increases by 1.5 times every 5 yr.

Time	Value of Investment
Initial	$800
5 yr	$1200
10 yr	$1800
15 yr	$2700
20 yr	■
25 yr	■
■	■
■	■

2. The number of animals doubles every 3 mo.

Time	Number of Animals
Initial	18
3 mo	36
6 mo	72
9 mo	■
12 mo	■
■	■
■	■
■	■

3. The amount of matter halves every year.

Time	Amount of Matter
Initial	3200 g
1 yr	1600 g
2 yr	800 g
3 yr	■
■	■
■	■
■	■

Evaluate each function for the domain {1, 2, 4, 5}.

4. $y = 2^x$

5. $y = 3.1^x$

6. $y = 0.8^x$

7. $y = 2 \cdot 4^x$

8. $y = 10 \cdot 3^x$

9. $y = 25 \cdot 5^x$

10. $y = \left(\frac{2}{3}\right)^x$

11. $y = 100\left(\frac{1}{10}\right)^x$

12. $y = \frac{1}{4} \cdot 8^x$

Graph each function.

13. $y = 3^x$

14. $y = 6^x$

15. $y = 1.5^x$

16. $y = 7^x$

17. $y = 10 \cdot 5^x$

18. $y = 16 \cdot 0.5^x$

19. $y = \frac{1}{8} \cdot 2^x$

20. $y = \frac{1}{2} \cdot 4^x$

21. $y = 8\left(\frac{5}{2}\right)^x$

Evaluate each function.

22. $y = 5.5^x$ for $x = 1, 3,$ and 4

23. $y = 4 \cdot 1.5^x$ for $x = 2, 4,$ and 5

24. $y = 3 \cdot 4^x$ for $x = 1, 3,$ and 5

25. $y = 6^x$ for $x = 2, 3,$ and 4

26. $y = 0.7^x$ for $x = 1, 3,$ and 4

27. $y = 3.1^x$ for $x = 1, 2,$ and 3

28. $y = 500 \cdot 0.5^x$ for $x = 1, 4,$ and 5

29. $y = 5000 \cdot 0.1^x$ for $x = 2, 4,$ and 8

30. $y = 5.5^x$ for $x = 2, 3,$ and 4

31. $y = 2^x$ for $x = 4, 8,$ and 10

32. $y = 128 \cdot 0.25^x$ for $x = 2, 3$ and 4

33. $y = 25 \cdot 4^x$ for $x = 3, 4,$ and 6

Practice 8-2
• •
Example Exercises

Example 1

Write an exponential function to model each situation. Find each amount after the specified time.

1. Suppose a new automobile currently costs $10,000. The cost of a new automobile increases 5% per year. Determine what the cost of a new car would be after each of the following years.

   a. 1 yr   **b.** 2 yr   **c.** 5 yr   **d.** 7 yr

2. The population of a city of 450,000 people increases 2.5% per year. Determine what the population of that city would be after each of the following years.

   a. 1 yr   **b.** 3 yr   **c.** 6 yr   **d.** 10 yr

Example 2

Write an exponential function to model each situation. Find each amount after the specified time.

3. Suppose you invest $1000 in an account paying 5.5% interest compounded annually. Find the account balance after each of the following years.

   a. 1 yr   **b.** 5 yr   **c.** 10 yr   **d.** 20 yr

4. Suppose you invest $2500 in an account paying 7.25% interest compounded annually. Find the account balance after each of the following years.

   a. 1 yr   **b.** 2 yr   **c.** 6 yr   **d.** 25 yr

Example 3

Write an exponential function to model each situation. Find each amount after the specified time.

5. Suppose you invest $5000 in an account paying 5.5% interest. Find the account balance after 15 yr with the interest compounded the following ways.

   a. annually   **b.** semi-annually   **c.** quarterly   **d.** daily

Practice 8-2
· ·
Mixed Exercises

Write an exponential function to model each situation. Find each amount after the specified time.

1. Suppose one of your ancestors invested $500 in 1700 in an account paying 4% interest compounded annually. Find the account balance after each of the following dates.

   a. 1750   **b.** 1800   **c.** 1900   **d.** 2000

2. Suppose you invest $1500 in an account paying 4.75% interest. Find the account balance after 25 yr with the interest compounded the following ways.

   a. annually   **b.** semi-annually   **c.** quarterly   **d.** monthly

3. The starting salary for a new employee is $25,000. The salary for this employee increases by 8% per year. What is the salary after each of the following years?

   a. 1 yr   **b.** 3 yr   **c.** 5 yr   **d.** 15 yr

4. Suppose you invest $750 in an account paying 5.25% interest compounded annually. Find the account balance after each of the following years.

   a. 3 yr   **b.** 5 yr   **c.** 7 yr   **d.** 18 yr

5. The tax revenue that a small city receives increases by 3.5% per year. In 1980, the city received $250,000 in tax revenue. Determine the tax revenue after each of the following dates.

   a. 1985   **b.** 1988   **c.** 1990   **d.** 1996

6. Suppose your grandmother invested $500 in 1960 at 7%. Find the account balance in 1995 with the interest compounded the following ways.

   a. semi-annually   **b.** quarterly   **c.** monthly   **d.** daily

7. The population of a city of 120,000 people increases by 1.05% per year. Determine what the population of the city is after each of the following years.

   a. 1 yr   **b.** 2 yr   **c.** 4 yr   **d.** 8 yr

8. Suppose you invest $1200 in an account paying 6% interest compounded quarterly. Find the account balance after each of the following years.

   a. 2 yr   **b.** 5 yr   **c.** 10 yr   **d.** 25 yr

· ·

Practice 8-3

• •

Example Exercises

Example 1

Use the graph to answer each exercise.

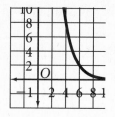

1. What is the value of the function when $x = 4$?

2. What is the value of the function when $x = 6$?

3. When is the value of the function 4?

Example 2

Use a table of values to graph each function.

4. $y = 10 \cdot 0.9^x$ 5. $y = 4.5 \cdot 0.95^x$ 6. $f(x) = 100 \cdot 0.1^x$

7. $y = 90 \cdot 0.8^x$ 8. $y = 30 \cdot 0.85^x$ 9. $g(x) = 100 \cdot 0.99^x$

10. $y = 512 \cdot \left(\frac{1}{2}\right)^x$ 11. $y = 64 \cdot \left(\frac{3}{4}\right)^x$ 12. $y = 27 \cdot \left(\frac{2}{3}\right)^x$

Example 3

Calculate the percent of decrease for each decay factor.

13. 0.9   14. 0.85   15. 0.09   16. 0.72

17. 0.58   18. 0.998   19. 0.53   20. 0.01

Calculate the decay factor for each percent of decrease.

21. 75%   22. 1.5%   23. 4%   24. 18.2%

25. 0.5%   26. 83%   27. 7.2%   28. 3.8%

Write an exponential function to model each situation. Find each amount after the specified time.

29. A city of 140,000 people has a 1% annual decrease in population. Determine the city's population after each of the following years.

   a. 2 yr   **b.** 5 yr   **c.** 10 yr   **d.** 20 yr

30. A $6000 investment has a 8.5% loss each year. Determine the value of the investment after each of the following years.

   a. 1 yr   **b.** 3 yr   **c.** 5 yr   **d.** 8 yr

Practice 8-3
• •
Mixed Exercises

Use the graph to answer each exercise.

1. What is the value of the function when $x = 3$?

2. What is the value of the function when $x = 4$?

3. When is the value of the function 2?

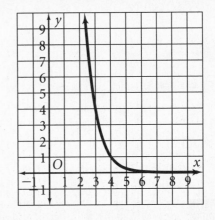

Find the percent of decrease for each decay factor.

4. 0.92   **5.** 0.75   **6.** 0.04   **7.** 0.995

8. 0.73   **9.** 0.18   **10.** 0.65   **11.** 0.025

Write an exponential function to model each situation. Find each amount after the specified time.

12. Suppose the acreage of forest is decreasing by 2% per year because of development. If there are currently 4,500,000 acres of forest, determine the amount of forest land after each of the following years.

    a. 3 yr   **b.** 5 yr   **c.** 10 yr   **d.** 20 yr

13. A $10,500 investment has a 15% loss each year. Determine the value of the investment after each of the following years.

    a. 1 yr   **b.** 2 yr   **c.** 4 yr   **d.** 10 yr

14. A city of 2,950,000 people has a 2.5% annual decrease in population. Determine the city's population after each of the following years.

    a. 1 yr   **b.** 5 yr   **c.** 15 yr   **d.** 25 yr

15. A $25,000 purchase has a 12% decrease in value per year. Determine the value of the purchase after each of the following years.

    a. 1 yr   **b.** 3 yr   **c.** 5 yr   **d.** 7 yr

Use a table of values to graph each function.

16. $y = 18 \cdot 0.98^x$ **17.** $y = 8.5 \cdot 0.998^x$ **18.** $f(x) = 48 \cdot 0.625^x$

19. $y = 50 \cdot 0.875^x$ **20.** $y = 6 \cdot 0.95^x$ **21.** $g(x) = 25 \cdot 0.2^x$

22. $y = 36 \cdot \left(\frac{1}{3}\right)^x$ **23.** $y = 15 \cdot \left(\frac{3}{5}\right)^x$ **24.** $y = 9 \cdot \left(\frac{8}{9}\right)^x$

Practice 8-4

· ·

Example Exercises

Example 1

Simplify each expression.

1. 3^0 **2.** 6^0 **3.** -4^0 **4.** $(-9)^0$ **5.** 5.45^0

Evaluate each function for $t = 0$.

6. $f(t) = 75 \cdot 3^t$ **7.** $f(t) = 25 \cdot 7^t$ **8.** $f(t) = -6 \cdot 2.5^t$ **9.** $f(t) = 5.9 \cdot 10^t$

Example 2

Write each expression as a simple fraction.

10. 6^{-2} **11.** 5^{-4} **12.** 8^{-3} **13.** 10^{-2} **14.** 7^{-1}

15. 9^{-2} **16.** 8^{-1} **17.** $(-4)^{-2}$ **18.** $(-2)^{-2}$ **19.** $(-13)^{-1}$

20. -6^{-3} **21.** -3^{-2} **22.** 4^{-5} **23.** 11^{-2} **24.** -5^{-3}

Example 3

Rewrite each expression so that all exponents are positive.

25. $2x^{-3}$ **26.** $-4y^{-2}$ **27.** $6ab^{-2}$ **28.** $-3x^{-1}y$ **29.** $2v^{-2}w^{-3}$

30. $\dfrac{1}{x^{-4}}$ **31.** $\dfrac{3}{x^{-2}}$ **32.** $\dfrac{5}{st^{-2}}$ **33.** $\dfrac{6f}{g^{-1}}$ **34.** $\dfrac{-2k^3}{j^{-4}h^{-7}}$

35. $\dfrac{a^{-2}}{b^{-3}}$ **36.** $\dfrac{m^{-4}}{n^{-1}}$ **37.** $\dfrac{x^2y^{-3}}{z^{-5}}$ **38.** $\dfrac{4d^{-4}e^{-1}}{f^{-8}}$ **39.** $\dfrac{2}{a^2b^{-3}}$

Example 4

Use a graphing calculator to graph each function over the domain
$\{-2 \le x \le 2\}$.

40. $y = 3^x$ **41.** $y = -3^x$ **42.** $y = \left(\frac{1}{3}\right)^x$ **43.** $y = -\left(\frac{1}{3}\right)^x$

44. $y = \left(\frac{3}{4}\right)^x$ **45.** $y = -\left(\frac{1}{2}\right)^x$ **46.** $y = \left(\frac{5}{2}\right)^x$ **47.** $y = -\left(\frac{3}{2}\right)^x$

48. $y = 2 \cdot 2^x$ **49.** $y = \frac{1}{2} \cdot 2^x$ **50.** $y = 2\left(\frac{1}{2}\right)^x$ **51.** $y = \frac{1}{4}\left(\frac{1}{2}\right)^x$

52. $y = 3 \cdot (1.5)^x$ **53.** $y = -2 \cdot (2.5)^x$ **54.** $y = 0.5 \cdot 4^x$ **55.** $y = 2.5 \cdot 2^x$

Practice 8-4

· ·

Mixed Exercises

Write each expression as an integer or a simple fraction.

1. 16^0

2. 4^{-2}

3. 3^{-3}

4. 8^{-4}

5. $\frac{1}{2^{-5}}$

6. $\frac{4}{4^{-3}}$

7. $\frac{3}{6^{-1}}$

8. $\frac{1}{2^{-5}}$

9. $3 \cdot 8^0$

10. $16 \cdot 2^{-2}$

11. 12^{-1}

12. -7^{-2}

13. $16 \cdot 4^0$

14. 9^0

15. $\frac{32^{-1}}{8^{-1}}$

16. $\frac{9}{2^{-1}}$

17. $\frac{8^{-2}}{4^0}$

18. $\frac{9^{-1}}{3^{-2}}$

19. $5(-6)^0$

20. 3.7^0

21. $(-9)^{-2}$

22. $(-4.9)^0$

23. $-6 \cdot 3^{-4}$

24. $\frac{7^{-2}}{4^{-1}}$

Evaluate each expression for $m = 4$, $n = 5$, and $p = -2$.

25. m^p

26. n^m

27. p^p

28. n^p

29. $m^p n$

30. m^{-n}

31. p^{-n}

32. mn^p

33. p^{-m}

34. $\frac{m}{n^p}$

35. $\frac{1}{n^{-m}}$

36. $-n^{-m}$

Rewrite each expression so that all exponents are positive.

37. x^{-8}

38. xy^{-3}

39. $a^{-5}b$

40. $m^2 n^{-9}$

41. $\frac{1}{x^{-7}}$

42. $\frac{3}{a^{-4}}$

43. $\frac{5}{d^{-3}}$

44. $\frac{6}{r^{-5}s^{-1}}$

45. $3x^{-6}y^{-5}$

46. $8a^{-3}b^2c^{-2}$

47. $15s^{-9}t^{-1}$

48. $-7p^{-5}q^{-3}r^2$

49. $\frac{d^{-4}}{e^{-7}}$

50. $\frac{3m^{-4}}{n^{-8}}$

51. $\frac{6m^{-8}n}{p^{-1}}$

52. $\frac{a^{-2}b^{-1}}{cd^{-3}}$

Use a graphing calculator to graph each function over the domain $\{-2 \le x \le 2\}$.

53. $y = 2^x$

54. $y = -2^x$

55. $y = \left(\frac{1}{2}\right)^x$

56. $y = -\left(\frac{1}{2}\right)^x$

57. $y = 2 \cdot 4^x$

58. $y = \frac{1}{2} \cdot 4^x$

59. $y = -\left(\frac{3}{4}\right)^x$

60. $y = -3 \cdot 2^x$

61. $y = (1.1)^x$

62. $y = \frac{3}{4} \cdot 3^x$

63. $y = -2 \cdot 3^x$

64. $y = -4\left(\frac{1}{2}\right)^x$

65. $y = 2(3.5)^x$

66. $y = \left(\frac{2}{5}\right)^x$

67. $y = 5(0.5)^x$

68. $y = 7\left(\frac{1}{4}\right)^x$

Practice 8-5

• •

Example Exercises

Example 1

Write each number in scientific notation.

1. 7,100,000
2. 18,900,000,000
3. 0.000 03
4. 0.000 000 068

5. 120 billion
6. 4.5 million
7. 8 ten-thousandths
8. 375 millionths

9. 25×10^5
10. 76×10^{-4}
11. 0.025×10^9
12. 0.98×10^{-3}

Write each number in standard notation.

13. 6×10^3
14. 8×10^{-3}
15. 4.5×10^4
16. 2.9×10^{-6}

17. 8.01×10^{-4}
18. 9.075×10^8
19. 1.0092×10^6
20. 5.045×10^{-7}

21. 17.8×10^4
22. 31.9×10^{-2}
23. 0.002×10^{-3}
24. 0.098×10^7

Example 2

Simplify. Give each answer in scientific notation.

25. $5 \times (3.2 \times 10^6)$
26. $(6.4 \times 10^6) \div 8$
27. $8 \times (4.1 \times 10^{-2})$

28. $(4.5 \times 10^{-5}) \div 9$
29. $3 \times (7.4 \times 10^7)$
30. $(4.2 \times 10^{-3}) \div 6$

31. $(9.3 \times 10^9) \div 3$
32. $2 \times (3.7 \times 10^{-5})$
33. $2.1 \times (6 \times 10^3)$

34. $15 \times (4 \times 10^{-7})$
35. $(1.8 \times 10^{-8}) \div 9$
36. $(2.4 \times 10^5) \div 8$

37. $(3.2 \times 10^{-4}) \div 8$
38. $5 \times (4.1 \times 10^{-3})$
39. $(3.5 \times 10^{10}) \div 5$

Example 3

Simplify. Give each answer in scientific notation rounded to the nearest hundredth.

40. $(3.5 \times 10^8)(7.1 \times 10^2)$
41. $\dfrac{7.52 \times 10^{10}}{3.9 \times 10^4}$
42. $(5.1 \times 10^{10})(6.79 \times 10^{-4})$

43. $(4.16 \times 10^{-3})(7.7 \times 10^{-4})$
44. $\dfrac{8.015 \times 10^6}{1.754 \times 10^{11}}$
45. $\dfrac{3.013 \times 10^{-6}}{7.187 \times 10^{-13}}$

46. $\dfrac{5.72 \times 10^3}{6.11 \times 10^{-4}}$
47. $(9.28 \times 10^{-9})(3.75 \times 10^6)$
48. $\dfrac{9.97 \times 10^{-3}}{8.01 \times 10^5}$

49. $(6.1 \times 10^{15})(5.32 \times 10^{-8})$
50. $\dfrac{5.125 \times 10^6}{1.927 \times 10^{-3}}$
51. $(4.87 \times 10^{-15})(3.9 \times 10^{12})$

52. $\dfrac{3.975 \times 10^9}{2.15 \times 10^7}$
53. $(5.75 \times 10^7)(1.98 \times 10^{-5})$
54. $(7.9 \times 10^{-13})(6.41 \times 10^{10})$

Practice 8-5
• •

Mixed Exercises

Write each number in standard notation.

1. 7×10^4 **2.** 3×10^{-2} **3.** 2.6×10^5 **4.** 7.1×10^{-4}

5. 5.71×10^{-5} **6.** 4.155×10^7 **7.** 3.0107×10^2 **8.** 9.407×10^{-5}

9. 31.3×10^6 **10.** 83.7×10^{-4} **11.** 0.018×10^{-1} **12.** 0.016×10^5

13. 8.0023×10^{-3} **14.** 6.902×10^8 **15.** 1005×10^2 **16.** 0.095×10^{-1}

Write each number in scientific notation.

17. 51,000,000   **18.** 975,000,000,000   **19.** 0.000 000 12   **20.** 0.000 005 008

21. 1560 billion   **22.** 0.5 million   **23.** 2 thousandths   **24.** 1095 millionths

25. 194×10^3 **26.** 154×10^{-3} **27.** 0.05×10^6 **28.** 0.031×10^{-4}

29. 790 thousand   **30.** 25 hundredths   **31.** 0.000 000 000 159   **32.** 5,000,900,000,000

Simplify. Give each answer in scientific notation rounded to the nearest hundredth when necessary.

33. $(3 \times 10^{-4})(5 \times 10^6)$ **34.** $(8 \times 10^{-4}) \div 2$ **35.** $4 \times (3 \times 10^5)$

36. $5 \times (7 \times 10^{-2})$ **37.** $(2.8 \times 10^{-5})(5 \times 10^7)$ **38.** $(7.5 \times 10^{-4}) \div 5$

39. $(1.6 \times 10^5) \div 4$ **40.** $\dfrac{6.8 \times 10^{10}}{3.7 \times 10^4}$ **41.** $(6.2 \times 10^{-9})(1.91 \times 10^3)$

42. $\dfrac{5.3 \times 10^5}{6.9 \times 10^8}$ **43.** $8 \times (9 \times 10^9)$ **44.** $(6 \times 10^{-6}) \div 8$

45. $7 \times (9 \times 10^6)$ **46.** $\dfrac{7.13 \times 10^3}{1.92 \times 10^{-4}}$ **47.** $\dfrac{8.175 \times 10^{-4}}{3.792 \times 10^{-8}}$

48. $(2.7 \times 10^9) \div 9$ **49.** $(4.12 \times 10^3)(7.38 \times 10^5)$ **50.** $3 \times (1.2 \times 10^{-4})$

51. $\dfrac{5.3 \times 10^5}{6.9 \times 10^8}$ **52.** $(7.13 \times 10^{-3})(1.7 \times 10^{-7})$ **53.** $(3.11 \times 10^{-2})(2.7 \times 10^{-4})$

54. $2 \times (6.1 \times 10^{-8})$ **55.** $(3.9 \times 10^{-1})(8.2 \times 10^4)$ **56.** $(8.4 \times 10^{-9}) \div 4$

57. $(3.7 \times 10^{-4})(7.25 \times 10^{10})$ **58.** $\dfrac{4.785 \times 10^{-9}}{8.131 \times 10^{-6}}$ **59.** $\dfrac{2.9 \times 10^{-10}}{7.85 \times 10^{-15}}$

60. $(6.3 \times 10^8) \div 7$ **61.** $\dfrac{3.918 \times 10^8}{4.382 \times 10^{-2}}$ **62.** $3 \times (3.2 \times 10^{-2})$

63. $(9.2 \times 10^8)(2.7 \times 10^{10})$ **64.** $(8.7 \times 10^{-2})(7.7 \times 10^{-5})$ **65.** $\dfrac{9.72 \times 10^{-8}}{3.89 \times 10^{-6}}$

Practice 8-6
• •
Example Exercises

Example 1

Simplify each expression.

1. $a^2 \cdot a^3$ **2.** $b^4 \cdot b^6$ **3.** $x^5 \cdot x$ **4.** $5^2 \cdot 5^4$

5. $m^3 \cdot n^4 \cdot m^5$ **6.** $x^2 \cdot y^3 \cdot y^2 \cdot x$ **7.** $p^3 \cdot q^5 \cdot p^7$ **8.** $s^4 \cdot t^5 \cdot t^3$

9. $(3m^3)(2m^5)$ **10.** $(-5m^2)(-2m^4)$ **11.** $4^3 \cdot 4^4$ **12.** $(6p^5)(8p^4)$

13. $(2x^2y)(3xy^4)$ **14.** $(-2a^2b^3)(3a^4)$ **15.** $(5x^2y^3)(-2x^4y^5)$ **16.** $(3m^2n^5)(-8mn^2)$

Example 2

Simplify. Give the answer in scientific notation.

17. $(2 \times 10^3)(4 \times 10^5)$ **18.** $(3.5 \times 10^5)(2 \times 10^9)$ **19.** $(8 \times 10^{11})(2.5 \times 10^3)$

20. $3(4 \times 10^5)(5 \times 10^3)$ **21.** $200(5 \times 10^3)(1 \times 10^7)$ **22.** $(9 \times 10^8)(0.2 \times 10^4)$

23. The speed of light is approximately 1.86×10^5 mi/s. If it takes light from the sun 5.1×10^2 s to reach the earth, how far away is the sun?

24. One liter equals 1×10^6 mm^3. There are 5×10^6 red blood cells in 1 mm^3 of human blood. How many red blood cells are there in 1 L of human blood?

25. Suppose you are an astronaut on a mission to Mars. Your spacecraft is traveling at a speed of 2.5×10^4 mi/h. It takes you 5.5×10^3 h to reach Mars. How many miles do you travel?

Example 3

Simplify each expression. Use only positive exponents.

26. $m^8 \cdot m^{-5}$ **27.** $r^3 \cdot r^{-2}$ **28.** $a^{-5} \cdot a^3$ **29.** $x^{-4} \cdot x^{-7} \cdot x^5$

30. $n^{-3} \cdot n^{-4}$ **31.** $(2a^{-3})(5a^4)$ **32.** $(-3p^{-5})(2p^8)$ **33.** $s^3 \cdot s^{-5} \cdot s^7$

34. $\dfrac{1}{b^{-8} \cdot b^{-1}}$ **35.** $\dfrac{1}{x^3 \cdot x^{-7}}$ **36.** $\dfrac{1}{y^{-5} \cdot y^8}$ **37.** $\dfrac{1}{m \cdot m^{-3}}$

Simplify. Give the answer in scientific notation.

38. $(2 \times 10^{-4})(5 \times 10^2)$ **39.** $(3 \times 10^{-2})(4 \times 10^{-3})$ **40.** $(8 \times 10^5)(7 \times 10^{-2})$

41. $(6 \times 10^8)(7 \times 10^{-12})$ **42.** $(7.5 \times 10^{-1})(2 \times 10^3)$ **43.** $(2 \times 10^{13})(3.6 \times 10^{-9})$

44. $(4 \times 10^6)(2.5 \times 10^{-3})$ **45.** $(4.6 \times 10^{-3})(3 \times 10^{-1})$ **46.** $(3.4 \times 10^{-11})(4 \times 10^{-8})$

Practice 8-6

· ·

Mixed Exercises

Simplify each expression. Use only positive exponents.

1. $(3d^{-4})(5d^8)$ **2.** $(-8m^4)(4m^8)$ **3.** $n^{-6} \cdot n^{-9}$

4. $a^3 \cdot a$ **5.** $k^8 \cdot k^5$ **6.** $(3p^{-15})(6p^{11})$

7. $p^7 \cdot q^5 \cdot p^6$ **8.** $(-1.5a^5b^2)(6a)$ **9.** $(-2d^3e^3)(6d^4e^6)$

10. $\dfrac{1}{b^{-7} \cdot b^5}$ **11.** $p^5 \cdot q^2 \cdot p^4$ **12.** $\dfrac{1}{n^6 \cdot n^{-5}}$

13. $(8d^4)(4d^7)$ **14.** $x^{-9} \cdot x^3 \cdot x^2$ **15.** $2^3 \cdot 2^2$

16. $r^7 \cdot s^4 \cdot s \cdot r^3$ **17.** $b^7 \cdot b^{13}$ **18.** $(7p^4)(5p^9)$

19. $s^8 \cdot s^{-9} \cdot s^3$ **20.** $(6r^4s^3)(9rs^2)$ **21.** $4^3 \cdot 4^2$

22. $m^{12} \cdot m^{-14}$ **23.** $s^7 \cdot t^4 \cdot t^8$ **24.** $(-3xy^6)(3.2x^5y)$

25. $a^{-7} \cdot a^9$ **26.** $\dfrac{1}{h^7 \cdot h^3}$ **27.** $\dfrac{1}{t^{-5} \cdot t^{-3}}$

28. $f^5 \cdot f^2 \cdot f^0$ **29.** $r^6 \cdot r^{-13}$ **30.** $5^{-6} \cdot 5^4$

Simplify. Give the answer in scientific notation.

31. $(7 \times 10^7)(5 \times 10^{-5})$ **32.** $5(3 \times 10^8)(3 \times 10^4)$ **33.** $(9.5 \times 10^{-4})(2 \times 10^{-5})$

34. $(4 \times 10^9)(4.1 \times 10^8)$ **35.** $(7.2 \times 10^{-7})(2 \times 10^{-5})$ **36.** $13(5 \times 10^7)(4 \times 10^3)$

37. $(6 \times 10^{-6})(5.2 \times 10^4)$ **38.** $(4 \times 10^6)(9 \times 10^8)$ **39.** $(6.1 \times 10^9)(8 \times 10^{14})$

40. $(2.1 \times 10^{-4})(4 \times 10^{-7})$ **41.** $(1.6 \times 10^5)(3 \times 10^{11})$ **42.** $(9 \times 10^{12})(0.3 \times 10^{-18})$

43. $2(4 \times 10^9)(11 \times 10^3)$ **44.** $(5 \times 10^{13})(9 \times 10^{-9})$ **45.** $10(7 \times 10^6)(4 \times 10^9)$

46. $(6 \times 10^{-8})(12 \times 10^{-7})$ **47.** $(6 \times 10^{15})(3.2 \times 10^2)$ **48.** $(5 \times 10^8)(2.6 \times 10^{-16})$

49. In 1990, the St. Louis metropolitan area had an average of $82 \times 10^{-6}\,\text{g/m}^3$ of pollutants in the air. How many grams of pollutants were there in $2 \times 10^3\,\text{m}^3$ of air?

50. Light will travel approximately 5.88×10^{12} mi in one year. This is called a light-year. Suppose a star is 2×10^4 light-years away. How many miles is it to that star?

51. The weight of $1\,\text{m}^3$ of air is approximately 1.3×10^3 g. Suppose that the volume of air inside of a building is $3 \times 10^6\,\text{m}^3$. How much does the air inside the building weigh?

52. Light will travel 1.18×10^{10} in. in 1 s. How far will light travel in 1 nanosecond, 1×10^{-9} s?

Practice 8-7

• •

Example Exercises

Example 1

Simplify each expression. Use positive exponents.

1. $(x^2)^3$ **2.** $(a^4)^2$ **3.** $(2^3)^2$ **4.** $(d^3)^{-2}$

5. $(b^{-7})^2$ **6.** $(m^{-2})^{-4}$ **7.** $(3^{-2})^2$ **8.** $x^2 \cdot (x^2)^5$

9. $(y^3)^4$ **10.** $d^2 \cdot (d^3)^4$ **11.** $n^8 \cdot (n^{-2})^2$ **12.** $(a^3)^{-3} \cdot a^5$

13. $3^2 \cdot (3^2)^2$ **14.** $x \cdot (x^4)^6$ **15.** $b^{-3} \cdot (b^2)^3$ **16.** $(y^3)^{-5} \cdot y^{20}$

Example 2

Simplify each expression. Use positive exponents.

17. $(xy)^3$ **18.** $(x^2y)^4$ **19.** $(m^{-2}n^3)^{-2}$

20. $(5a^3)^2$ **21.** $(7b^{-1})^2$ **22.** $(2a^2b^3)^2$

23. $a^3 \cdot (a^2b)^4$ **24.** $(x^{-2})^3(x^2y^3)^4$ **25.** $(6x^2)^2(3x^2y)^3$

26. $(m^2)^{-4}(m^2n^3)^2$ **27.** $(x^3y^2)^2(xy^3)^4$ **28.** $(a^2b^3)^{-1}(a^{-2}b)^{-5}$

Example 3

Multiply. Give your answers in scientific notation.

29. $(3 \times 10^4)^3$ **30.** $(3 \times 10^{-5})^2$ **31.** $(8 \times 10^{10})^2$

32. $(4 \times 10^{-7})^2$ **33.** $(6 \times 10^7)^3$ **34.** $(2 \times 10^3)^5$

35. $(2 \times 10^6)^{-2}$ **36.** $10^3 \cdot (5 \times 10^8)^2$ **37.** $10^2 \cdot (6 \times 10^9)^2$

38. $10^{-4} \cdot (3 \times 10^4)^2$ **39.** $10^{-7} \cdot (5 \times 10^3)^3$ **40.** $(10^5)^2(8 \times 10^{-4})^2$

41. The Earth is shaped somewhat like a sphere. The volume of a sphere can be calculated by using the formula $V = \frac{4}{3}\pi r^3$. The radius of the Earth is 2.1×10^7 ft. What is the volume of the Earth?

42. The volume of a cylindrical water storage tank can be calculated by using the formula $V = 3.14r^2h$. The radius of the tank is 1×10^2 ft. The height of the tank is 5×10^1 ft. What is the volume of the tank?

43. The kinetic energy, in joules, of a moving object can be found by using the formula $E = \frac{1}{2}mv^2$, where m is the mass and v is the speed of the object. The mass of a proton is 1.67×10^{-27} kg. Find the kinetic energy of a proton traveling 2.5×10^8 m/s.

Practice 8-7

Mixed Exercises

Simplify each expression. Use positive exponents.

1. $(4a^5)^3$

2. $(2^{-3})^4$

3. $(m^{-3}n^4)^{-4}$

4. $(x^5)^2$

5. $2^5 \cdot (2^4)^2$

6. $(4x^4)^3(2xy^3)^2$

7. $x^4 \cdot (x^4)^3$

8. $(x^5y^3)^3(xy^5)^2$

9. $(5^2)^2$

10. $(a^4)^{-5} \cdot a^{13}$

11. $(3f^4g^{-3})^3(f^2g^{-2})^{-1}$

12. $x^3 \cdot (x^3)^5$

13. $(d^2)^{-4}$

14. $(a^3b^4)^{-2}(a^{-3}b^{-5})^{-4}$

15. $(x^2y)^4$

16. $(12b^{-2})^2$

17. $(m^{-5})^{-3}$

18. $(x^{-4})^5(x^3y^2)^5$

19. $(y^6)^{-3} \cdot y^{21}$

20. $n^6 \cdot (n^{-2})^5$

21. $(m^5)^{-3}(m^4n^5)^4$

22. $(a^3)^6$

23. $b^{-9} \cdot (b^2)^4$

24. $(4^{-1}s^3)^{-2}$

25. $(5a^3b^5)^4$

26. $(b^{-3})^6$

27. $(y^6)^3$

28. $a^{-4} \cdot (a^4b^3)^2$

29. $(x^4y)^3$

30. $d^3 \cdot (d^2)^5$

Multiply. Give your answers in scientific notation.

31. $10^{-9} \cdot (2 \times 10^2)^2$

32. $(3 \times 10^{-6})^3$

33. $10^4 \cdot (4 \times 10^6)^3$

34. $(9 \times 10^7)^2$

35. $10^{-3} \cdot (2 \times 10^3)^5$

36. $(7 \times 10^5)^3$

37. $(5 \times 10^5)^4$

38. $(2 \times 10^{-3})^3$

39. $(5 \times 10^2)^{-3}$

40. $(3 \times 10^5)^4$

41. $(4 \times 10^8)^{-3}$

42. $(1 \times 10^{-5})^{-5}$

43. $10^5 \cdot (8 \times 10^7)^3$

44. $(10^2)^3(6 \times 10^{-3})^3$

45. $10^7 \cdot (2 \times 10^2)^4$

46. The kinetic energy, in joules, of a moving object is found by using the formula $E = \frac{1}{2}mv^2$, where m is the mass and v is the speed of the object. The mass of a car is 1.59×10^3 kg. The car is traveling at 2.7×10^1 m/s. What is the kinetic energy of the car?

47. The moon is shaped somewhat like a sphere. The surface area of the moon is found by using the formula $S = 12.56r^2$. What is the surface area of the moon if the radius is 1.08×10^3 mi?

48. Because of a record corn harvest, excess corn is stored on the ground in a pile. The pile is shaped liked a cone. The height of the pile is 25 ft and the radius of the pile is 1.2×10^2 ft. Use the formula $V = \frac{1}{3}\pi r^2 h$ to find the volume.

49. The distance in feet that an object travels in t seconds is given by the formula $d = 64t^2$. How far has the object traveled after 1.5×10^3 s?

Practice 8-8

· ·

Example Exercises

Example 1

Simplify each expression. Use only positive exponents.

1. $\dfrac{2^5}{2^3}$ 2. $\dfrac{5^4}{5^7}$ 3. $\dfrac{a^{10}}{a^7}$ 4. $\dfrac{x^{12}}{x^8}$

5. $\dfrac{m^5 n^2}{m^8 n^7}$ 6. $\dfrac{xy^6}{x^4 y^3}$ 7. $\dfrac{a^3 b^4}{ab^2}$ 8. $\dfrac{3^{-2}}{3^2}$

9. $\dfrac{6^{-3}}{6^{-5}}$ 10. $\dfrac{d^{-3}}{d^{-9}}$ 11. $\dfrac{a^{-6}}{a^4}$ 12. $\dfrac{x^{10}}{x^{-7}}$

13. $\dfrac{a^4 b^{-7} c}{a^8 b^3 c^{-6}}$ 14. $\dfrac{s^{-14}}{s^{-10}}$ 15. $\dfrac{a^2 b^{-3}}{a^{-4} b^3}$ 16. $\dfrac{p^{-4} q^{-6}}{pq^{-1}}$

Example 2

Simplify each expression. Give your answer in scientific notation.

17. $\dfrac{5 \times 10^6}{2.5 \times 10^4}$ 18. $\dfrac{8.4 \times 10^8}{4 \times 10^3}$ 19. $\dfrac{7.2 \times 10^3}{8 \times 10^{-5}}$ 20. $\dfrac{2.8 \times 10^{-3}}{7 \times 10^{-9}}$

21. $\dfrac{4.7 \times 10^{10}}{3.2 \times 10^6}$ 22. $\dfrac{3.9 \times 10^6}{5.7 \times 10^{10}}$ 23. $\dfrac{4.71 \times 10^3}{6.13 \times 10^{-3}}$ 24. $\dfrac{7.91 \times 10^{-6}}{4.43 \times 10^{-4}}$

25. $\dfrac{525 \text{ billion}}{355 \text{ million}}$ 26. $\dfrac{25 \text{ million}}{65 \text{ million}}$ 27. $\dfrac{21.6 \text{ million}}{537.1 \text{ million}}$ 28. $\dfrac{905 \text{ million}}{6.1 \text{ million}}$

Example 3

Simplify each expression. Use only positive exponents.

29. $\left(\dfrac{3}{4}\right)^2$ 30. $\left(\dfrac{4}{a^2}\right)^4$ 31. $\left(\dfrac{3}{x^3}\right)^4$ 32. $\left(\dfrac{3}{5}\right)^{-3}$

33. $\left(-\dfrac{4}{3^2}\right)^{-2}$ 34. $\left(\dfrac{a^4}{b}\right)^3$ 35. $\left(\dfrac{x^{-3}}{y^{-2}}\right)^{-1}$ 36. $\left(\dfrac{a^2 b}{c^3}\right)^4$

37. $\left(\dfrac{2x^3 y^2}{z}\right)^2$ 38. $\left(\dfrac{3a^{-2} b^3}{c^{-4}}\right)^3$ 39. $\left(\dfrac{x^4 y^0}{z^{-3}}\right)^{-2}$ 40. $\left(\dfrac{8a^2 b^{-1}}{c^4}\right)^0$

41. $\left(\dfrac{2^3 m^2 n^{-2}}{p^{-4}}\right)^2$ 42. $\left(\dfrac{a^3 b^4}{a^5}\right)^3$ 43. $\left(\dfrac{2x^4 y^{-3}}{x^2 y^4}\right)^0$ 44. $\left(\dfrac{p^3 q^{-2}}{q^2 r^{-4}}\right)^1$

Practice 8-8

• •

Mixed Exercises

Simplify each expression. Use only positive exponents.

1. $\dfrac{c^{15}}{c^9}$

2. $\left(\dfrac{x^3 y^{-2}}{z^{-5}}\right)^{-4}$

3. $\dfrac{x^7 y^9 z^3}{x^4 y^7 z^8}$

4. $\left(\dfrac{a^2}{b^3}\right)^5$

5. $\dfrac{3^7}{3^4}$

6. $\left(\dfrac{a^3}{b^2}\right)^4$

7. $\left(\dfrac{2}{3}\right)^{-2}$

8. $\left(\dfrac{p^{-3} q^{-2}}{q^{-3} r^5}\right)^4$

9. $\dfrac{a^6 b^{-5}}{a^{-2} b^7}$

10. $\dfrac{7^{-4}}{7^{-7}}$

11. $\dfrac{a^7 b^6}{a^5 b}$

12. $\left(\dfrac{a^2 b^{-4}}{b^2}\right)^5$

13. $\left(-\dfrac{3}{2^3}\right)^{-2}$

14. $\dfrac{z^7}{z^{-3}}$

15. $\left(\dfrac{5 a^0 b^4}{c^{-3}}\right)^2$

16. $\dfrac{x^4 y^{-8} z^{-2}}{x^{-1} y^6 z^{-10}}$

17. $\dfrac{m^6}{m^{10}}$

18. $\left(\dfrac{2^3 m^4 n^{-1}}{p^2}\right)^0$

19. $\left(\dfrac{s^{-4}}{t^{-1}}\right)^{-2}$

20. $\left(\dfrac{2 a^3 b^{-2}}{c^3}\right)^5$

21. $\left(\dfrac{x^{-3} y}{x z^{-4}}\right)^{-2}$

22. $\dfrac{h^{-13}}{h^{-8}}$

23. $\dfrac{4^6}{4^8}$

24. $\left(\dfrac{1}{3}\right)^3$

25. $\dfrac{x^5 y^3}{x^2 y^9}$

26. $\left(\dfrac{m^{-3} n^4}{n^{-2}}\right)^4$

27. $\dfrac{4^{-1}}{4^2}$

28. $\left(\dfrac{a^8 b^6}{a^{11}}\right)^5$

29. $\dfrac{n^9}{n^{15}}$

30. $\left(\dfrac{r^3 s^{-1}}{r^2 s^6}\right)^{-1}$

31. $\dfrac{n^{-8}}{n^4}$

32. $\dfrac{m^8 n^3}{m^{10} n^5}$

Simplify each expression. Give your answer in scientific notation.

33. $\dfrac{3.54 \times 10^{-9}}{6.15 \times 10^{-5}}$

34. $\dfrac{9.35 \times 10^{-3}}{3.71 \times 10^{-5}}$

35. $\dfrac{495 \text{ billion}}{23.9 \text{ million}}$

36. $\dfrac{8 \times 10^9}{4 \times 10^5}$

37. $\dfrac{9.5 \times 10^9}{5 \times 10^{12}}$

38. $\dfrac{6.4 \times 10^9}{8 \times 10^7}$

39. $\dfrac{298 \text{ billion}}{49 \text{ million}}$

40. $\dfrac{1.8 \times 10^{-8}}{0.9 \times 10^3}$

41. $\dfrac{3.6 \times 10^6}{9 \times 10^{-3}}$

42. $\dfrac{8.19 \times 10^7}{4.76 \times 10^{-2}}$

43. $\dfrac{65 \text{ million}}{19.5 \text{ billion}}$

44. $\dfrac{4.9 \times 10^{12}}{7 \times 10^3}$

45. $\dfrac{36.2 \text{ trillion}}{98.5 \text{ billion}}$

46. $\dfrac{3.9 \times 10^3}{1.3 \times 10^8}$

47. $\dfrac{5.6 \times 10^{-5}}{8 \times 10^{-7}}$

48. $\dfrac{40 \text{ million}}{985 \text{ million}}$

Chapter Project Manager

• •

Chapter 8 Moldy Oldies

Getting Started Read about the project on page 361 of your textbook. To get started on the project, you will need a sheet of 1-mm grid paper, a packet of unflavored gelatin, a flat dish or plate, a small piece of unprocessed cheese, and plastic wrap. As you work on the project, you will need a calculator and materials on which you will record your calculations and make your graphs. Keep all of your work for the project in a folder, along with this Project Manager.

Checklist and Suggestions

❑ Start mold growth. (p. 366)   Follow directions carefully.

❑ Record mold growth for ten days. (p. 372)   Only count squares completely covered by mold.

❑ Make scatter plot of growth data. (p. 389)   Accurately label scatter plots.

❑ Compare scatter plot with others. (p. 389)   Think of reasons for differences in scatter plots.

❑ Find percent of growth for each day. (p. 395)   Start on first day that mold covers one square.

❑ Average daily percent of growth. (p. 395)   Use average as base for exponential function.

❑ Graph exponential function. (p. 395)   Graph function on scatter plot.

❑ Use function to predict growth. (p. 400)   Predict growth for the next two weeks.

❑ Compare predictions with growth. (p. 400)   Discuss deviations from prediction.

Scoring Rubric

3 You follow all directions for preparing the experiment. Your exponential function is reasonably consistent with actual growth. The graph and the scatter plot are neat, accurate, and clearly show the relationship between the actual and predicted growth.

2 You follow most directions for preparing the experiment, with few errors. Your exponential function is somewhat consistent with actual growth. Your graph and the scatter plot generally show the relationship between actual and predicted growth, with minor errors in scale.

1 You make errors preparing the experiment. The relationship between your exponential function and the actual growth is unclear. Your graph and scatter plot are not accurate.

0 You leave out or do not complete important parts.

Your Evaluation of Project Evaluate your work, based on the *Scoring Rubric*.

Teacher's Evaluation of Project

✔ Checkpoint 1

• •

For use after 8-3

Write an exponential function to model each situation. Find each amount after the specified time.

1. $16,000 loan balance
16% decrease each year
7 yr

2. $5000 initial investment
triples every 15 yr
60 yr

3. 175,000 initial population
2.5% increase each year
12 yr

4. In 1944, the U.S. Coast Guard released 29 reindeer on a small island west of Alaska. Due to plentiful food and a lack of predators the reindeer population grew rapidly.

    a. Suppose the reindeer population increased 32.4% each year. Write a function to model the growth of the island's reindeer population.

    b. The reindeer population reached a maximum in 1963. Estimate the maximum reindeer population using the function from part **a**.

Graph each function. Label each graph as *exponential growth* or *exponential decay*.

5. $y = 3 \cdot 0.4^x$

6. $y = \left(\frac{1}{15}\right) \cdot 3^x$

7. $f(x) = 5 \cdot \left(\frac{5}{4}\right)^x$

- - - - ✂ -

✔ Checkpoint 2

• •

For use after 8-6

Write each expression as an integer or simple fraction.

1. 11^0

2. $(-3)^2$

3. -4^3

4. $\left(\frac{3}{4}\right)^{-1}$

5. $(-5)^3$

6. $-\left(\frac{2}{3}\right)^{-2}$

7. Standardized Test Prep Which expression can be simplified as $\frac{6m^4}{n^7}$?

    A. $(6mn)(m^4n^{-7})$ **B.** $(2mn^{-5})(4m^3n^{-2})$ **C.** $(2m^6n^{10})(3m^{-2}n^{-3})$ **D.** $(3m^{-1}n^2)(3m^5n^{-9})$

Mental Math Simplify. Give your answers in scientific notation.

8. $(8 \times 10^8) \times 6$

9. $7 \times (5 \times 10^3)$

10. $(4 \times 10^3) \times 0.6$

11. $(6 \times 10^{-11}) \div 2$

12. The average distance from Earth to the sun is 149,600,000 km.
The average distance from Mars to the sun is 227,900,000 km.

    a. Write each number in scientific notation.

    b. Find the distance between Earth and Mars.

• •

Chapter Assessment

Form A

Chapter 8

Evaluate each function for $x = -1, 1, 2.$

1. $f(x) = 4 \cdot 7^x$ **2.** $y = \frac{2}{3} \cdot 6^x$ **3.** $f(x) = 13 \cdot (1.3)^x$ **4.** $h(x) = 3 \cdot \left(\frac{4}{5}\right)^x$

5. An investment of \$2000 doubles every 12 yr.

    a. How much is the investment worth after 36 yr? After 60 yr?

    b. Model the value of the investment with an exponential function.

6. The decay of 50 g of the radioactive substance cobalt-60 can be modeled by the exponential function $y = 50 \cdot 0.88^x$, where x is in years.

    a. Graph the exponential function.

    b. Use your graph to estimate the half-life of cobalt-60.

7. **Open-ended** Write and solve a problem comparing interest compounded annually to interest compounded quarterly.

8. **Critical Thinking** In the exponential decay equation $y = 7 \cdot 0.5^x$, is there a value of x that makes y less than zero? Explain.

9. **Standardized Test Prep** If $z = \frac{1}{2}$, which expression has the greatest value?

    A. $z^{-6}z^4$ **B.** $(z^{-2}z^5)^{-2}$ **C.** $(z^3)^5$ **D.** $-(z^2z^{-4})^{-3}$

Graph each function

10. $f(x) = \frac{1}{3} \cdot 3^x$ **11.** $y = 3 \cdot \frac{1}{3}^x$ **12.** $y = 0.5^x$

13. For what values of x is the function $y = 3^x$ between zero and one? For what values of x is the function less than zero?

Chapter Assessment (continued) **Form A**

Chapter 8

Solve each problem using scientific notation.

14. At the end of 1993 there were 109 nuclear power plants operating in the United States. These plants generated a total of 6,520,000,000,000,000 Btu (British thermal unit) of electric power in 1993. How much energy was generated per plant?

15. A red blood cell is 0.000007 m in diameter. There are about 20,000,000,000,000 red blood cells in a 125-lb person. If all of the red blood cells were lined up end to end, how long would they be?

Determine whether each number is in scientific notation. If it is not, write it in scientific notation.

16. 4.8×10^4 **17.** 119×10^{-3} **18.** -7×10^{11} **19.** $\frac{4}{5} \times 10^2$

Simplify each expression. Use positive exponents.

20. $a^4 b^{-7} c^0$ **21.** $(0.93^6)(0.93^{-8})$ **22.** $\frac{p^3 q^{-1}}{q^2 r^{-6}}$

23. $(m^3 n^{-5} m^{-1})^{-3}$ **24.** $\left(\frac{x^4 y^{-2}}{x^{-3} y^5} \right)^{-1}$ **25.** $u^{-5} v^4 (-u^3 v^{-2})^3$

26. Suppose you deposit $1000 earned from your summer job in a savings account that pays 4.8% interest compounded monthly.

    a. Write an exponential function to model the amount of money in your savings account.

    b. How much will you have in your account after 1 yr? After 2 yr?

27. The function $y = 41 \cdot 0.95^x$ models the difference (in minutes) between men's and women's finishing times for the Boston Marathon. The number of years since women first officially ran the race in 1972 is represented by x.

    a. Does the exponential function represent growth or decay?

    b. Estimate the difference between finishing times in 1990.

    c. Predict the difference between finishing times in 2002.

Chapter Assessment

Form B

Chapter 8

Evaluate each function for $x = -2, 1, 3$.

1. $f(x) = 2 \cdot 4^x$ **2.** $y = \frac{3}{4} \cdot 8^x$ **3.** $f(x) = 16 \cdot (0.5)^x$ **4.** $h(x) = 4 \cdot \left(\frac{4}{3}\right)^x$

5. A population of bacteria triples in size every 5 h.

    a. If the initial population of the bacteria is 125 cells, what will the population be after 15 h? After 25 h?

    b. Model the bacteria population with an exponential function.

6. The decay of 16 g of the radioactive substance neptunium-239 can be modeled by the exponential function $y = 16 \cdot 0.74^x$, where x is in days.

    a. Graph the exponential function.

    b. Use your graph to estimate the half-life of neptunium-239.

7. **Open-ended** Describe a situation that can be modeled by the exponential function $y = 1500 \cdot 0.95^x$.

8. **Writing** Explain how you can tell when a number written in scientific notation is greater than one, and when it is less than one.

9. **Standardized Test Prep** If p is a positive integer greater than 1, which expression has the greatest value?

    A. $(p^4 p^{-5})^2$ **B.** $-p(p^2)^5$ **C.** $3p^4 p^0$ **D.** $(p^{-3} p^{-4})^{-1}$

Graph each function.

10. $y = \frac{1}{4} \cdot 4^x$ **11.** $f(x) = 4 \cdot \left(\frac{1}{4}\right)^x$ **12.** $y = 2^{-x}$

13. Benjamin wrote $4^{-3} = (-4)(-4)(-4) = -64$. Samantha wrote $4^{-3} = \frac{1}{4^3} = \frac{1}{64}$. Whose work is correct? Explain.

Chapter Assessment (continued)   Form B

Chapter 8

Solve each problem using scientific notation.

14. In 1989, the supertanker *Exxon Valdez* spilled 9,415,000 gal of oil into Prince William Sound, Alaska. Daily oil consumption in the United States in 1989 was about 706,000,000 gal. How many spills the size of the *Exxon Valdez* would it take to equal one day's consumption?

15. The state of Colorado covers about 104,000 mi^2. The Indian Ocean covers about 28,000,000 mi^2. How many Colorados would it take to cover the Indian Ocean?

Determine whether each number is in scientific notation. If it is not, write it in scientific notation.

16. 6.1×10^{-7} **17.** 44×10^5 **18.** 0.32×10^{11} **19.** 3.4×10^1

Simplify each expression. Use positive exponents.

20. $x^3 y^{-3} z^4$ **21.** $\dfrac{r^{-2} s^6}{r^3 s^5}$ **22.** $2a^{-2}(ab^0)^3$

23. $(-7.1^7)(7.1^{-5})$ **24.** $(6m^0)(3^{-1} m^2 n^{-4})$ **25.** $\dfrac{3 j^3 k^{-5} l}{2 j^{-3} k^{-5} l^4}$

26. Suppose you win $500 in an essay contest and put the money in a savings account. The account pays 6.4% compounded quarterly.

     a. Model the amount in the savings account with an exponential function.

     b. How much money is in the account after 2 yr? After 5 yr?

27. The function $y = 35,000 \cdot 0.96^x$ models the population of a city since 1980.

     a. Determine whether the function models exponential growth or decay, and find the growth or decay factor.

     b. Using this function estimate the population of the city 10 yr ago.

     c. Predict the population of the city 10 yr from now.

Alternative Assessment
Chapter 8

Give complete answers.

TASK 1

Write, solve, and graph two problems using an exponential function
$(y = a \cdot b^x)$. One problem is to model exponential growth using
compound interest. The second problem needs to model exponential
decay using half-life models.

TASK 2

Choose a fraction and an integer to use as values for the variable m. Find the
values of m^{-3}, m^2, m^{-1}, and $m^{-2} \cdot \dfrac{1}{m^2}$.

Alternative Assessment (continued)

Chapter 8

TASK 3

Explain how you decide when to use scientific notation in a problem. As part of your explanation, write and solve a problem that supports your reasoning.

TASK 4

Suppose you are a math teacher and you have just taught a lesson on exponents. A student asks you to review some problems she did. Look over the problems and correct any mistakes that she made.

a.
$$\frac{4a^2b^5}{2a^6b^2} = \frac{4}{2} \cdot \frac{a^2}{a^6} \cdot \frac{b^5}{b^2}$$
$$= 2 \cdot a^4 \cdot b^3$$
$$= 2a^4b^3$$

b.
$$\frac{y^2}{y^7} = y^{-14}$$
$$= \frac{1}{y^{14}}$$

c.
$$\frac{12k^2m^3n}{-9m^3n^6k^5} = \frac{12}{-9} \cdot \frac{k^2}{k^5} \cdot \frac{m^3}{m^3} \cdot \frac{n^6}{n}$$
$$= \frac{-4}{3} \cdot k^{-3} \cdot m^3 \cdot n^5$$
$$= \frac{-4m^3n^5}{k^3}$$

d. $2x^2y \cdot 3x^5y^2 = (2 \cdot 3)(x^2 \cdot x^5)(y \cdot y^2)$
$$= 6x^{10}y^2$$

e. $(3x^2)^3 \cdot 2x^4 = 3x^8 \cdot 2x^4$
$$= 6x^{32}$$

Name _____ Class _____ Date _____

Cumulative Review
Chapter 8
•••

For Exercises 1–13, choose the correct letter.

1. Which values of a and b are a solution to the inequality $|5 - 2a| - b \le 4$?

   A. $a = 6, b = -2$ **B.** $a = -4, b = 3$ **C.** $a = 3, b = -1$ **D.** $a = -3, b = 5$

2. What is the value of the function $y = -x^2 + 6x - 5$ when $x = 4$?

   A. 3   **B.** 35   **C.** 5   **D.** –3

3. Which equation has a slope of $-\frac{1}{2}$ and a graph that passes through $(-3, 4)$?

   A. $y = -\frac{1}{2}x + 4$ **B.** $4y + 3x = -2$ **C.** $2y = x + 8$ **D.** $2y + x = 5$

4. Choose the correct mean, median and mode for the following set of data: 22, 20, 35, 20, 15, 25, 20, 35.

   A. mean = 20; median = 24; mode = 21   **B.** mean = 24; median = 21; mode = 20

   C. mean = 25; median = 22; mode = 35   **D.** mean = 21; median = 20; mode = 24

5. Use the quadratic formula to find the solutions of $-3x^2 + 10x - 8 = 0$.

   A. $-\frac{3}{4}, 2$ **B.** $\frac{4}{3}, -2$ **C.** $\frac{4}{3}, 2$ **D.** $4, \frac{2}{3}$

6. Which of the following is the graph of $2y - 3x = 8$?

   A.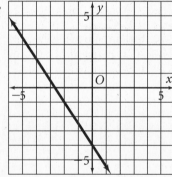

   B.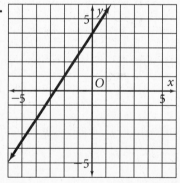

   C.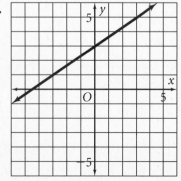

   D.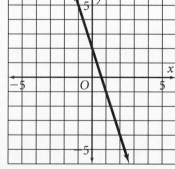

Cumulative Review (continued)
Chapter 8

7. Which value of x is a solution of both $2(x - 8) < 5$ and $-4(2 - x) \geq 1$?

   A. 3   **B.** –4   **C.** 0   **D.** 2

8. Find the solution to the system of equations.
$$x - 3y = -4$$
$$2x + y = 6$$

   A. $(-3, 2)$ **B.** $(0, 6)$ **C.** $\left(-\frac{2}{7}, 5\right)$ **D.** $(2, 2)$

9. A fishing guide charges \$25/h for the first 4 h and \$15 for each additional hour. Isabella paid the fishing guide \$175. How many hours was Isabella fishing?

   A. 5 h   **B.** 9 h   **C.** 7 h   **D.** 8 h

10. A bag contains seven red apples and nine green apples. What is the probability of choosing a green apple and then a red apple without replacing?

   A. $\frac{9}{7}$ **B.** $\frac{63}{256}$ **C.** $\frac{21}{80}$ **D.** $\frac{2}{3}$

11. Which function does *not* have a discriminant of 12?

   A. $-x^2 + 6x - 6 = 0$ **B.** $x^2 + 2x + 5 = 0$

   C. $x^2 + 4x + 1 = 0$ **D.** $x^2 - 8x + 13 = 0$

12. Which product is greatest?

   A. $(4.2 \times 10^{-3})(6.9 \times 10^9)$ **B.** $(3.7 \times 10^5)(4.8 \times 10^{-2})$

   C. $(5.1 \times 10^3)(5.1 \times 10^3)$ **D.** $(7.3 \times 10^{10})(2.5 \times 10^{-5})$

13. The graph of a system of linear equations is two parallel lines. How many solutions does the system have?

   A. infinitely many   **B.** one   **C.** none

   D. cannot be determined from the information provided

14. The circle at the center of a basketball court has an area of 113 ft^2. What is the radius of the circle in feet?

   A. 5 ft   **B.** 6 ft   **C.** 7 ft   **D.** 11 ft

Find each answer.

15. Find the vertex and x-intercepts of $f(x) = x^2 - 5x + 4$.

16. **Open-ended** Write and solve a problem involving compound interest.

17. Solve the system of inequalities by graphing.
$$y > -2x + 3$$
$$y \leq 3x - 2$$

Standardized Test Practice

Chapter 8

For Exercises 1–11, choose the correct letter.

1. Which of the following is a graph of an exponential function?

A.

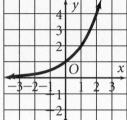

B.

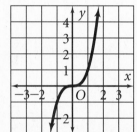

C.

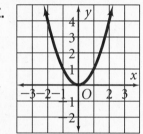

D.

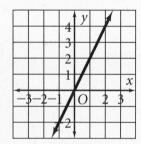

    E. none of the above

2. On January 1, 1997, you deposit $200.00 in a bank account paying 5% interest compounded annually on December 31 of each year. Which of the following will be the account balance on January 1, 2005?

  A. $281.42   **B.** $310.27

  C. $295.49   **D.** $781.25

  E. $512.59

3. Which of the following equations models exponential decay?

  A. $y = \frac{1}{4} \cdot 500^x$

  B. $\frac{1}{3}y = 6 \cdot 100^x$

  C. $y = 0.5 \cdot 8^x$

  D. $y = 23 \cdot \left(\frac{1}{2}\right)^x$

  E. $y = 0.004 \cdot 2^x$

4. The population of a city can be modeled using the equation $p = 40{,}000 \cdot \left(\frac{9}{10}\right)^x$. One year, the population was 23,620. Which of the following was the population a year later?

  A. 21,258   **B.** 27,620

  C. 19,620   **D.** 32,142

  E. 17,283

5. Which of the following is true?

  A. $\frac{x^{-3}}{x} = \frac{x}{x^4}$

  B. $\frac{y^2}{y^0}$ is undefined

  C. $\frac{b^5 c^{-2} d^4}{b^6 c d^{-2}} = \frac{d^8}{b c^3}$

  D. $\frac{f^2 g^{-3} h^3}{f^4 g^2 h^{-4}} = \frac{h^7}{f^2 g^5}$

  E. none of the above

6. Which of the following is the smallest number?

  A. $17{,}426 \times 10^{-1}$

  B. 181.823×10^3

  C. 0.19×10^6

  D. 0.235×10^9

  E. 0.00312×10^{10}

Standardized Test Practice (continued)

Chapter 8

7. Which of the following is true?

   A. $\frac{z^6}{z^2} = z^3$ **B.** $\frac{y^{-4}}{y^2} = y^{-2}$

   C. $\frac{b^3}{b^5} = \frac{1}{b^{-2}}$ **D.** $\frac{d^8}{d^{-6}} = d^2$

   E. $\frac{x^0}{x^{-3}} = x^3$

8. Compare the amounts in Column A and Column B.

Column A	Column B
number of years needed for $500 to double in an account paying 5% compounded annually	number of years needed for $1000 to double in an account paying 2.5% compounded annually

   A. The quantity in Column A is greater.

   B. The quantity in Column B is greater.

   C. The two quantities are equal.

   D. The relationship cannot be determined on the basis of the information supplied.

9. Compare the numbers in Column A and Column B.

Column A	Column B
1.02^0	1.15^0

   A. The quantity in Column A is greater.

   B. The quantity in Column B is greater.

   C. The two quantities are equal.

   D. The relationship cannot be determined on the basis of the information supplied.

10. Compare the numbers in Column A and Column B.

Column A	Column B
86 million	8.6×10^7

    A. The quantity in Column A is greater.

    B. The quantity in Column B is greater.

    C. The two quantities are equal.

    D. The relationship cannot be determined on the basis of the information supplied.

11. Compare the expressions in Column A and Column B for $x = 30$.

Column A	Column B
8^x	7^x

    A. The quantity in Column A is greater.

    B. The quantity in Column B is greater.

    C. The two quantities are equal.

    D. The relationship cannot be determined on the basis of the information supplied.

For Exercises 12–16, write your answer.

12. An entry-level position pays $7.50/h. A 5% raise is given at the end of each year of employment. Write the exponential equation that could be used to model this situation.

13. **OPEN-ENDED** Write a problem that can be solved using an exponential decay function.

14. Simplify $(0.25 \times 10^6)(40 \times 10^3)$.

15. Simplify $(a^2b)^3 \cdot \left(\frac{b^4}{c}\right)^{-1} \cdot \left(\frac{a^5}{c^{-2}}\right)^2$.

16. Write the expression $\frac{a^{-2}c^5e^0}{b^2d^{-4}f^{-3}}$ using only positive exponents.

For Exercises 17–19, mark your answers in the free response grid.

17. Evaluate the expression $\frac{ca}{a^b + b^d}$ for $a = -1$, $b = 3$, $c = 2$, and $d = 1$.

18. Evaluate the expression $\frac{a^4b^6}{c^3} \cdot \frac{c^4a^3}{a^7b^2}$ for $a = 93$, $b = 5$, $c = 10$

19. Evaluate the expression $z(xy)^3$ for $x = 4$, $y = 5$, and $z = 6$.

Chapter 8

•••

Bubble Grid Answer Sheet for Standardized Test Practice

1. Ⓐ Ⓑ Ⓒ Ⓓ Ⓔ
2. Ⓐ Ⓑ Ⓒ Ⓓ Ⓔ
3. Ⓐ Ⓑ Ⓒ Ⓓ Ⓔ
4. Ⓐ Ⓑ Ⓒ Ⓓ Ⓔ
5. Ⓐ Ⓑ Ⓒ Ⓓ Ⓔ
6. Ⓐ Ⓑ Ⓒ Ⓓ Ⓔ
7. Ⓐ Ⓑ Ⓒ Ⓓ Ⓔ
8. Ⓐ Ⓑ Ⓒ Ⓓ
9. Ⓐ Ⓑ Ⓒ Ⓓ
10. Ⓐ Ⓑ Ⓒ Ⓓ
11. Ⓐ Ⓑ Ⓒ Ⓓ

12.

13.

14.

15.

16.

17.

⊕	⓪	⓪	⓪	⓪	⓪
⊖	①	①	①	①	①
	②	②	②	②	②
	③	③	③	③	③
	④	④	④	④	④
	⑤	⑤	⑤	⑤	⑤
	⑥	⑥	⑥	⑥	⑥
	⑦	⑦	⑦	⑦	⑦
	⑧	⑧	⑧	⑧	⑧
	⑨	⑨	⑨	⑨	⑨

18.

⊕	⓪	⓪	⓪	⓪	⓪
⊖	①	①	①	①	①
	②	②	②	②	②
	③	③	③	③	③
	④	④	④	④	④
	⑤	⑤	⑤	⑤	⑤
	⑥	⑥	⑥	⑥	⑥
	⑦	⑦	⑦	⑦	⑦
	⑧	⑧	⑧	⑧	⑧
	⑨	⑨	⑨	⑨	⑨

19.

⊕	⓪	⓪	⓪	⓪	⓪
⊖	①	①	①	①	①
	②	②	②	②	②
	③	③	③	③	③
	④	④	④	④	④
	⑤	⑤	⑤	⑤	⑤
	⑥	⑥	⑥	⑥	⑥
	⑦	⑦	⑦	⑦	⑦
	⑧	⑧	⑧	⑧	⑧
	⑨	⑨	⑨	⑨	⑨

Chapter 8 Answers

Alternative Activity 8-2A

1. $y = 4.9 + 0.8x$; linear function

2.

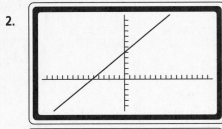

3.

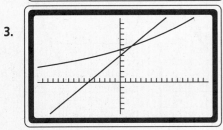

4. Job B is better paying for the first 3 yr. After 3 yr, Job A becomes better paying.

Alternative Activity 8-2B

1. $280.51 **2-4.** See below

	A	B	C	D
1	a	b	x	y
2	200	1.07	5	$280.51

5. $393.43 **6.** $431.78 **7.** 14.3 yr

Alternative Activity 8-4

1. 2 **2.** 4 **3.** 8 **4.** 16 **5.** 0.5 **6.** 0.25 **7.** 0.125 **8.** 0.0625

9. 0.5 **10.** 0.25 **11.** 0.125 **12.** 0.0625 **13.** $\frac{1}{2^5}$ **14.** 0.1; $\frac{1}{10^1}$

15. 0.01; $\frac{1}{10^2}$ **16.** 0.001; $\frac{1}{10^3}$ **17.** 0.0001; $\frac{1}{10^4}$

18. -0.5; $\frac{1}{(-2)^1}$ **19.** 0.25; $\frac{1}{(-2)^2}$ **20.** -0.125; $\frac{1}{(-2)^3}$

21. 0.0625; $\frac{1}{(-2)^4}$ **22.** -0.1; $-\frac{1}{10^1}$ **23.** -0.01; $-\frac{1}{10^2}$

24. -0.001; $-\frac{1}{10^3}$ **25.** -0.0001; $-\frac{1}{10^4}$ **26.** $\frac{1}{a^n}$ **27.** 1

28. 1 **29.** 1

Reteaching 8-1

1. 328,050 cans **2.** 67,500 **3.** $16,000 **4.** 1200; 76,800

Reteaching 8-2

1. 6720 **2.** $147 **3.** 4 ft

Reteaching 8-3

1. 0.4 **2.** 0.2 **3.** $\frac{4}{5}$ **4.** $y = 1.000 \cdot 0.90^5$; $590.49

5. $y = 5,000 \cdot 0.865^8$; $1567.11

6. $y = 20,000 \cdot 0.875^{10}$; 5262

Reteaching 8-4

1. $\frac{1}{1000}$ **2.** 1 **3.** $\frac{1}{625}$ **4.** $\frac{1}{343}$ **5.** $\frac{4}{9}$ **6.** $\frac{1}{625x^4}$

7. $\frac{1}{4}$ **8.** 1 **9.** $\frac{1}{b^5}$ **10.** $\left(\frac{7}{2}\right)^4$ **11.** $3a$ **12.** $\frac{1}{-4^3}$

13. $\frac{1}{a^3 a^4}$ **14.** $\frac{3}{x^2 y}$ **15.** $\frac{12x}{y^3}$ **16.** 128 **17.** $\frac{1}{12x}$

Reteaching 8-5

1. 4.2×10^5 **2.** 5.1×10^9 **3.** 2.6×10^{11} **4.** 8.3×10^8
5. 7.5×10^{-4} **6.** 4.005×10^{-3} **7.** 634,500,000 **8.** 0.000 032
9. 4,081,000 **10.** 0.002581

Reteaching 8-6

1. 5 **2.** 3 **3.** 3 **4.** 1 **5.** -1 **6.** -2 **7.** 12 **8.** 18 **9.** -9
10. $24x^6$ **11.** $18a^{-2}m^6$ **12.** $p^5 q^{-9}$

Reteaching 8-7

1. 390,625 **2.** a^{20} **3.** 64 **4.** $64x^3$ **5.** $49a^8$ **6.** $27g^6$
7. $g^{10}h^{15}$ **8.** s^{12} **9.** $x^6 y^{12}$ **10.** 1 **11.** g^2 **12.** c^{28} **13.** 1
14. $512a^3 b^{18}$

Reteaching 8-8

1. z^3 **2.** $\frac{729}{64}$ **3.** m **4.** $\frac{1}{5}$ **5.** b^6 **6.** $\frac{a^3}{3}$ **7.** $\frac{1}{8}$ **8.** d^5
9. x^2 **10.** 10^{18}

Chapter 8 Answers (continued)

Practice 8-1: Example Exercises

1.

Time	Number of Cells
Initial	100
1 h	200
2 h	400
3 h	800
4 h	1600
5 h	3200
6 h	6400

2.

Time	Investment Worth
Initial	$500
8 yr	$1000
16 yr	$2000
24 yr	$4000
32 yr	$8000
40 yr	$16,000
48 yr	$32,000

3.

Time	Number of Insects
Initial	20
2 mo	60
4 mo	180
6 mo	540
8 mo	1620
10 mo	4860
12 mo	14,580

4. 3; 9; 81 **5.** 4; 8; 32 **6.** 6.25; 15.625; 39.0625

7. 0.3; 0.0081; 0.002 43 **8.** 1600; 3200; 6400

9. 100; 25; 12.5 **10.** 54,000; 486,000

11. 125; 3125; 15,625 **12.** $\frac{1}{3}$; $\frac{1}{9}$; $\frac{1}{81}$ **13.** $\frac{2}{5}$; $\frac{4}{25}$; $\frac{8}{125}$

14. 512 **15.** 80; 64; $51\frac{1}{5}$

16.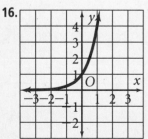

17.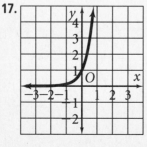

18.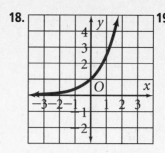

19.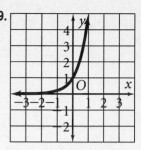

20.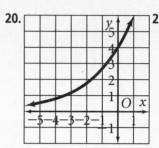

21.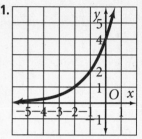

22.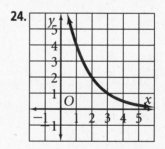

23.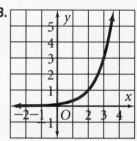

24.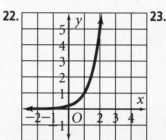

Practice 8-1: Mixed Exercises

1.

Time	Value of Investment
Initial	$800
5 yr	$1200
10 yr	$1800
15 yr	$2700
20 yr	$4050
25 yr	$6075
30 yr	$9112.50
35 yr	$13,668.75

2.

Time	Number of Animals
Initial	18
3 mo	36
6 mo	72
9 mo	144
12 mo	288
15 mo	576
18 mo	1152
21 mo	2304

3.

Time	Amount of Matter
Initial	3200 g
1 yr	1600 g
2 yr	800 g
3 yr	400 g
4 yr	200 g
5 yr	100 g
6 yr	50 g
7 yr	25 g

4. 2; 4; 16; 32   **5.** 3.1; 9.61; 92.3521; 286.29

6. 0.8; 0.64; 0.4096; 0.327 68   **7.** 8; 32; 512; 2048

8. 30; 90; 810; 2430   **9.** 125; 625; 15,625; 78,125

10. $\frac{2}{3}$; $\frac{4}{9}$; $\frac{16}{81}$; $\frac{32}{243}$

11. 10; 1; $\frac{1}{100}$; $\frac{1}{10,000}$ **12.** 2; 16; 1024; 8192

13. 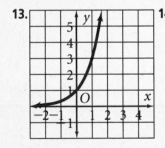   **14.**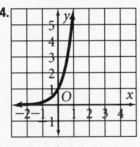

15. 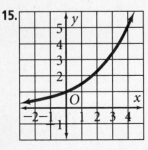   **16.**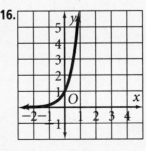

17. 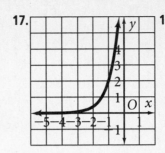   **18.**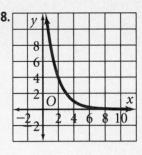

19. 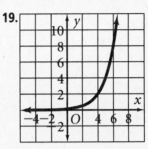   **20.**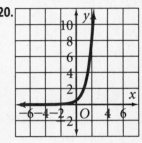

21.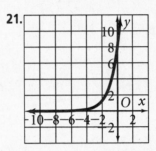

22. 5.5; 166.375; 915.0625   **23.** 9; 20.25; 30.375

24. 12; 192; 3072   **25.** 36; 216; 1296   **26.** 0.7; 0.343; 0.2401

27. 3.1; 9.61; 29.791   **28.** 250; 31.25; 15.625

29. 50; 0.5; 0.00005   **30.** 30.25; 166.375; 831.875

31. 16; 256; 1024   **32.** 8; 2; 0.5   **33.** 1600; 6400; 102,400

Practice 8-2: Example Exercises

1a. $10,500   **1b.** $11,025   **1c.** $12,762.82   **1d.** $14,071

2a. 461,250   **2b.** 484,601   **2c.** 521,862   **2d.** 576,038

3a. $1055   **3b.** $1306.96   **3c.** $1708.14   **3d.** $2917.76

4a. $2681.25   **4b.** $2875.64   **4c.** $3804.73   **4d.** $14,383.76

5a. $11,162.38   **5b.** $11,283.01

5c. $11,345.46   **5d.** $11,408.70

Practice 8-2: Mixed Exercises

1a. $3553.34   **1b.** $25,252.47
1c. $1,275,374.90   **1d.** $64,412,743.02
2a. $4785.66   **2b.** $4850.51
2c. $4884.02   **2d.** $4906.80
3a. $27,000   **3b.** $31,492.80
3c. $36,733.20   **3d.** $79,304.23
4a. $874.44   **4b.** $968.66
4c. $1073.04   **4d.** $1883.91
5a. $296,921.58   **5b.** $329,202.26
5c. $352,649.69   **5d.** $433,496.51
6a. $45,556.41   **6b.** $5672.68
6c. $5753.08   **6d.** $5792.81
7a. 121,260   **7b.** 122,533
7c. 125,120   **7d.** 130,458
8a. $1351.79   **8b.** $1616.23
8c. $2176.82   **8d.** $5318.45

Practice 8-3: Example Exercises

1. 8   **2.** 2   **3.** when $x = 5$

4.
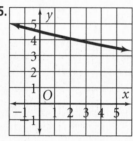

5.
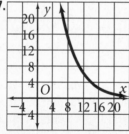

6.
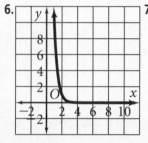

7.
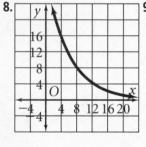

8.
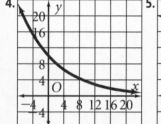

9.
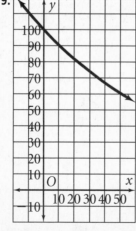

10.
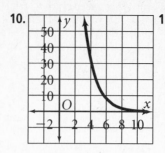

11.
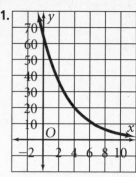

12.
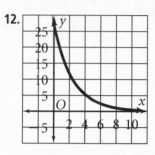

13. 10%   **14.** 15%   **15.** 91%   **16.** 28%   **17.** 42%   **18.** 0.2%
19. 47%   **20.** 99%   **21.** 0.25   **22.** 0.985   **23.** 0.96   **24.** 0.818
25. 0.995   **26.** 0.17   **27.** 0.928   **28.** 0.962
29a. 137,214   **29b.** 133,139   **29c.** 126,613   **29d.** 114,507
30a. $5490   **30b.** $4596.37   **30c.** $3848.19   **30d.** $2947.95

Practice 8-3: Mixed Exercises

1. 4   **2.** 1   **3.** when $x = 3.5$ **4.** 8%   **5.** 25%   **6.** 96%
7. 0.5%   **8.** 27%   **9.** 82%   **10.** 35%   **11.** 97.5%
12a. 4,235,364   **12b.** 4,067,644
12c. 3,676,828   **12d.** 3,004,236
13a. $8925   **13b.** $7586.25
13c. $5481.07   **13d.** $2067.18
14a. 2,876,250   **14b.** 2,599,232
14c. 2,017,861   **14d.** 1,566,525
15a. $22,000   **15b.** $17,036.80
15c. $13,193.30   **15d.** $10,216.89

16.
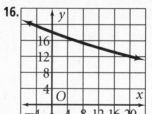

17.
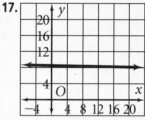

18.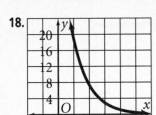

19.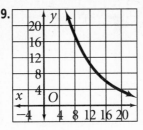

40.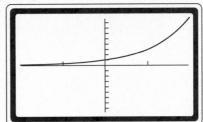

20.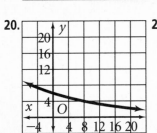

21.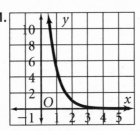

41.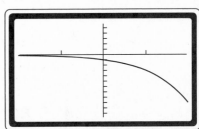

22.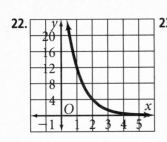

23.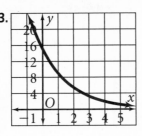

42.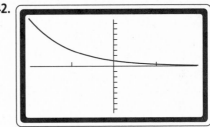

24.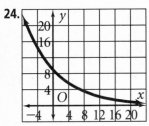

43.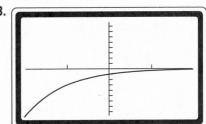

Practice 8-4: Example Exercises

1. 1   **2.** 1   **3.** −1   **4.** 1   **5.** 1   **6.** 75   **7.** 25   **8.** −6   **9.** 5.9

10. $\frac{1}{36}$ **11.** $\frac{1}{625}$ **12.** $\frac{1}{512}$ **13.** $\frac{1}{100}$ **14.** $\frac{1}{7}$ **15.** $\frac{1}{81}$

16. $\frac{1}{8}$ **17.** $\frac{1}{16}$ **18.** $\frac{1}{4}$ **19.** $-\frac{1}{13}$ **20.** $-\frac{1}{216}$

21. $-\frac{1}{9}$ **22.** $\frac{1}{1024}$ **23.** $\frac{1}{121}$ **24.** $-\frac{1}{125}$ **25.** $\frac{2}{x^3}$

26. $\frac{-4}{y^2}$ **27.** $\frac{6a}{b^2}$ **28.** $\frac{-3y}{x}$ **29.** $\frac{2}{v^2w^3}$ **30.** x^4

31. $3x^2$ **32.** $\frac{5t^2}{s}$ **33.** $6fg$ **34.** $-2h^7j^4k^3$ **35.** $\frac{b^3}{a^2}$

36. $\frac{n}{m^4}$ **37.** $\frac{x^2z^5}{y^3}$ **38.** $\frac{4f^8}{d^4e}$ **39.** $\frac{2b^3}{a^2}$

44.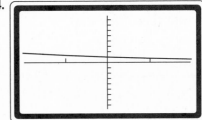

45.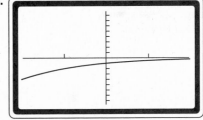

46.
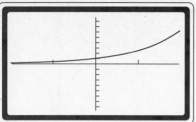

47.
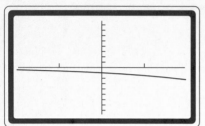

48.
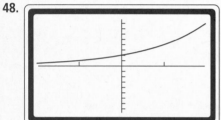

49.
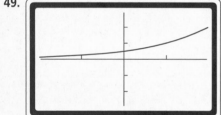

50.
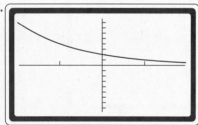

51.
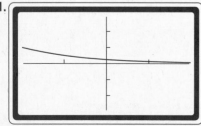

52.
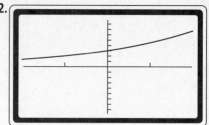

53.
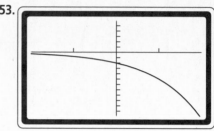

54.
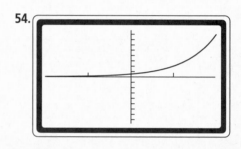

55.
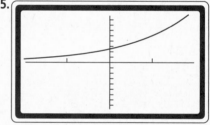

Practice 8-4: Mixed Exercises

1. 1 **2.** $\frac{1}{16}$ **3.** $\frac{1}{27}$ **4.** $\frac{1}{4096}$ **5.** 32 **6.** 256 **7.** 18 **8.** 32

9. 3 **10.** 4 **11.** $\frac{1}{12}$ **12.** $-\frac{1}{49}$ **13.** 16 **14.** 1 **15.** $\frac{1}{4}$

16. 18 **17.** $\frac{1}{64}$ **18.** 1 **19.** 5 **20.** 1 **21.** $\frac{1}{81}$ **22.** 1

23. $-\frac{2}{27}$ **24.** $\frac{4}{49}$ **25.** $\frac{1}{16}$ **26.** 625 **27.** $\frac{1}{4}$ **28.** $\frac{1}{25}$

29. $\frac{5}{16}$ **30.** $\frac{1}{1024}$ **31.** $-\frac{1}{32}$ **32.** $\frac{4}{25}$ **33.** $\frac{1}{16}$

34. 100 **35.** 625 **36.** $-\frac{1}{625}$ **37.** $\frac{1}{x^8}$ **38.** $\frac{x}{y^3}$ **39.** $\frac{b}{a^5}$

40. $\frac{m^2}{n^9}$ **41.** x^7 **42.** $3a^4$ **43.** $5d^3$ **44.** $6r^5s$ **45.** $\frac{3}{x^6 y^5}$

46. $\frac{8b^2}{a^3 c^2}$ **47.** $\frac{15}{s^9 t}$ **48.** $\frac{-7r^2}{p^5 q^3}$ **49.** $\frac{e^7}{d^4}$ **50.** $\frac{3n^8}{m^4}$

51. $\frac{6np}{m^8}$ **52.** $\frac{d^3}{a^2 bc}$

Chapter 8 Answers (continued)

53.

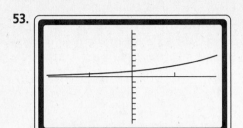

54.

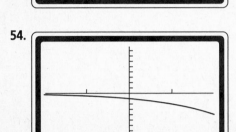

55.

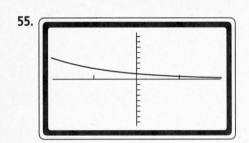

56.

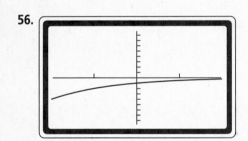

57.

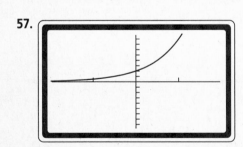

58.

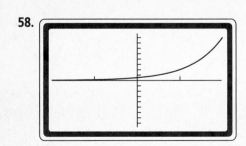

59.

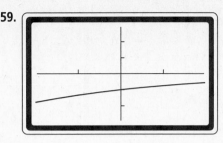

60.

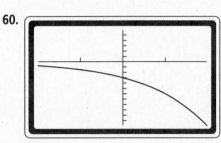

61.

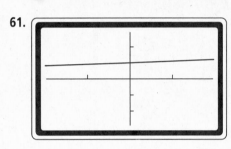

62.

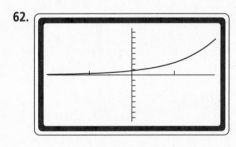

63.

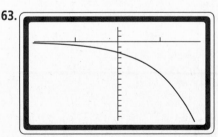

64.

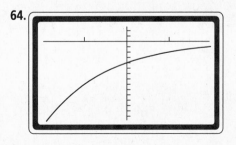

65.
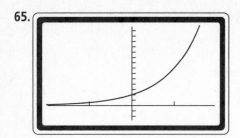

66.
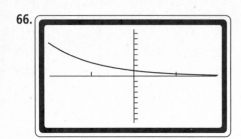

67.
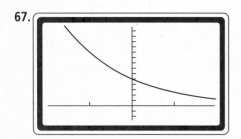

68.
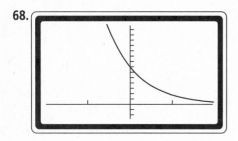

Practice 8-5: Example Exercises

1. 7.1×10^6 **2.** 1.89×10^{10} **3.** 3×10^{-5} **4.** 6.8×10^{-8}
5. 1.2×10^{11} **6.** 4.5×10^6 **7.** 8×10^{-5} **8.** 3.75×10^{-4}
9. 2.5×10^6 **10.** 7.6×10^{-3} **11.** 2.5×10^7
12. 9.8×10^{-4} **13.** 6,000 **14.** 0.008 **15.** 45,000
16. 0.000 002 9 **17.** 0.000 801 **18.** 907,500,000
19. 1,009,200 **20.** 0.000 000 504 5 **21.** 178,000 **22.** 0.319
23. 0.000 002 **24.** 980,000 **25.** 1.6×10^7 **26.** 8×10^5
27. 3.28×10^{-1} **28.** 5×10^{-6} **29.** 2.22×10^8
30. 7×10^{-4} **31.** 3.1×10^9 **32.** 7.4×10^{-5} .
33. 1.26×10^4 **34.** 6×10^{-6} **35.** 2×10^{-9}
36. 3×10^4 **37.** 4×10^{-5} **38.** 2.05×10^{-2}
39. 7×10^9 **40.** 2.49×10^{11} **41.** 1.93×10^6
42. 3.46×10^7 **43.** 3.20×10^{-6} **44.** 4.57×10^{-5}
45. 4.19×10^6 **46.** 9.36×10^6 **47.** 3.48×10^{-2}
48. 1.24×10^{-8} **49.** 3.25×10^8 **50.** 2.66×10^9
51. 1.90×10^{-2} **52.** 1.85×10^2 **53.** 1.14×10^3
54. 5.06×10^{-2}

Practice 8-5: Mixed Exercises

1. 70,000 **2.** 0.03 **3.** 260,000 **4.** 0.00071 **5.** 0.000 057 1
6. 41,550,000 **7.** 301.07 **8.** 0.000 094 07 **9.** 31,300,000
10. 0.00837 **11.** 0.0018 **12.** 1600 **13.** 0.0080023
14. 690,200,000 **15.** 100,500 **16.** 0.0095 **17.** 5.1×10^7
18. 9.75×10^{11} **19.** 1.2×10^{-7} **20.** 5.008×10^{-6}
21. 1.56×10^{12} **22.** 5×10^5 **23.** 2×10^{-3}
24. 1.095×10^{-3} **25.** 1.94×10^5 **26.** 1.54×10^{-1}
27. 5×10^4 **28.** 3.1×10^{-6} **29.** 7.9×10^5
30. 2.5×10^{-1} **31.** 1.59×10^{-10} **32.** 5.0009×10^{12}
33. 1.5×10^3 **34.** 4×10^{-4} **35.** 1.2×10^6
36. 3.5×10^{-1} **37.** 1.4×10^3 **38.** 1.5×10^{-4}
39. 4×10^4 **40.** 1.84×10^6 **41.** 1.18×10^{-5}
42. 7.68×10^{-4} **43.** 7.2×10^{10} **44.** 7.5×10^{-7}
45. 6.3×10^7 **46.** 3.71×10^7 **47.** 2.16×10^4
48. 3×10^8 **49.** 3.04×10^9 **50.** 3.6×10^{-4}
51. 7.68×10^{-4} **52.** 1.21×10^{-9} **53.** 8.40×10^{-6}
54. 1.22×10^{-7} **55.** 3.20×10^4 **56.** 2.1×10^{-9}
57. 2.68×10^7 **58.** 5.88×10^{-4} **59.** 3.69×10^4
60. 9×10^7 **61.** 8.94×10^9 **62.** 9.6×10^{-2}
63. 2.48×10^{19} **64.** 6.70×10^{-6} **65.** 2.50×10^{-2}

Practice 8-6: Example Exercises

1. a^5 **2.** b^{10} **3.** x^6 **4.** 5^6 **5.** $m^8 n^4$ **6.** $x^3 y^5$ **7.** $p^{10} q^5$
8. $s^4 t^8$ **9.** $6m^8$ **10.** $10m^6$ **11.** 4^7 **12.** $48p^9$ **13.** $6x^3 y^5$
14. $-6a^6 b^3$ **15.** $-10x^6 y^8$ **16.** $-24m^3 n^7$ **17.** 8×10^8
18. 7×10^{14} **19.** 2×10^{15} **20.** 6×10^9 **21.** 1×10^{13}
22. 1.8×10^{12} **23.** 9.486×10^7 mi **24.** 5×10^{12} red
blood cells **25.** 1.375×10^8 mi **26.** m^3 **27.** r **28.** $\dfrac{1}{a^2}$

29. $\dfrac{1}{x^6}$ **30.** $\dfrac{1}{n^7}$ **31.** $10a$ **32.** $-6p^3$ **33.** s^5 **34.** b^9 **35.** x^4

36. $\dfrac{1}{y^3}$ **37.** m^2 **38.** 1×10^{-1} **39.** 1.2×10^{-4}

40. 5.6×10^{-4} **41.** 4.2×10^{-3} **42.** 1.5×10^3

43. 7.2×10^4 **44.** 1×10^4 **45.** 1.38×10^{-3}

46. 1.36×10^{-18}

Chapter 8 Answers (continued)

Practice 8-6: Mixed Exercises

1. $15d^4$ 2. $-32m^{12}$ 3. $\frac{1}{n^{15}}$ 4. a^4 5. k^{13} 6. $\frac{18}{p^4}$

7. $p^{13}q^5$ 8. $-9a^6b^2$ 9. $-12d^7e^9$ 10. b^2 11. p^9q^2 12. $\frac{1}{n}$

13. $32d^{11}$ 14. $\frac{1}{x^4}$ 15. 2^5 16. $r^{10}s^5$ 17. b^{20} 18. $35p^{13}$

19. s^2 20. $54r^5s^5$ 21. 4^5 22. $\frac{1}{m^2}$ 23. s^7t^{12} 24. $-9.6x^6y^7$

25. a^2 26. $\frac{1}{h^{10}}$ 27. t^8 28. f^7 29. $\frac{1}{r^7}$ 30. $\frac{1}{5^2}$

31. 3.5×10^3 32. 4.5×10^{13} 33. 1.9×10^{-8}

34. 1.64×10^{18} 35. 1.44×10^{-11} 36. 2.6×10^{12}

37. 3.12×10^{-1} 38. 3.6×10^{15} 39. 4.88×10^{24}

40. 8.4×10^{-11} 41. 4.8×10^{16} 42. 2.7×10^{-6}

43. 8.8×10^{13} 44. 4.5×10^5 45. 2.8×10^{17}

46. 7.2×10^{-14} 47. 1.92×10^{18} 48. 1.3×10^{-7}

49. 1.64×10^{-1} g 50. 1.176×10^{17} mi

51. 3.9×10^9 g 52. 1.18×10^1 in.

Practice 8-7: Example Exercises

1. x^6 2. a^8 3. 2^6 4. $\frac{1}{d^6}$ 5. $\frac{1}{b^{14}}$ 6. m^8 7. $\frac{1}{3^4}$ 8. x^{12}

9. y^{12} 10. d^{14} 11. n^4 12. $\frac{1}{a^4}$ 13. 3^6 14. x^{25} 15. b^3

16. y^5 17. x^3y^3 18. x^8y^4 19. $\frac{m^4}{n^6}$ 20. $25a^6$ 21. $\frac{49}{b^2}$

22. $4a^4b^6$ 23. $a^{11}b^4$ 24. x^2y^{12} 25. $972x^{10}y^3$ 26. $\frac{n^6}{m^4}$

27. $x^{10}y^{16}$ 28. $\frac{a^8}{b^8}$ 29. 2.7×10^{13} 30. 9×10^{-10}

31. 6.4×10^{21} 32. 1.6×10^{-13} 33. 2.16×10^{23}

34. 3.2×10^{16} 35. 2.5×10^{-13} 36. 2.5×10^{20}

37. 3.6×10^{21} 38. 9×10^4 39. 1.25×10^4

40. 6.4×10^3 41. 3.88×10^{22} ft^3 42. 1.57×10^6 ft^3

43. 5.22×10^{-11} joules

Practice 8-7: Mixed Exercises

1. $64a^{15}$ 2. $\frac{1}{2^{12}}$ 3. $\frac{m^{12}}{n^{16}}$ 4. x^{10} 5. 2^{13} 6. $256x^{14}y^6$

7. x^{16} 8. $x^{17}y^{19}$ 9. 5^4 10. $\frac{1}{a^7}$ 11. $\frac{27f^{10}}{g^7}$ 12. x^{18}

13. $\frac{1}{d^8}$ 14. a^6b^{12} 15. x^8y^4 16. $\frac{144}{b^4}$ 17. m^{15} 18. $\frac{y^{10}}{x^5}$

19. y^3 20. $\frac{1}{n^4}$ 21. mn^{20} 22. a^{18} 23. $\frac{1}{b}$ 24. $\frac{16}{s^6}$

25. $625a^{12}b^{20}$ 26. $\frac{1}{b^{18}}$ 27. y^{18} 28. a^4b^6 29. $x^{12}y^3$

30. d^{13} 31. 4×10^{-5} 32. 2.7×10^{-17} 33. 6.4×10^{23}

34. 8.1×10^{15} 35. 3.2×10^{13} 36. 3.43×10^{17}

37. 6.25×10^{22} 38. 8×10^{-9} 39. 8×10^{-9}

40. 8.1×10^{21} 41. 1.5625×10^{-26} 42. 1×10^{25}

43. 5.12×10^{28} 44. 2.16×10^{-1} 45. 1.6×10^{16}

46. $5.795\,55 \times 10^5$ j 47. 1.46×10^7 mi^2

48. 3.8×10^5 ft^3 49. 1.44×10^8 ft

Practice 8-8: Example Exercises

1. 2^2 2. $\frac{1}{5^3}$ 3. a^3 4. x^4 5. $\frac{1}{m^3n^5}$ 6. $\frac{y^3}{x^3}$ 7. a^2b^2

8. $\frac{1}{3^4}$ 9. 6^2 10. d^6 11. $\frac{1}{a^{10}}$ 12. x^{17} 13. $\frac{c^7}{a^4b^{10}}$

14. $\frac{1}{s^4}$ 15. $\frac{a^6}{b^6}$ 16. $\frac{1}{p^5q^5}$ 17. 2×10^2 18. 2.1×10^5

19. 9×10^7 20. 4×10^5 21. 1.47×10^4

22. 6.84×10^{-5} 23. 7.68×10^5 24. 1.79×10^{-2}

25. 1.48×10^3 26. 3.85×10^{-1} 27. 4.02×10^1

28. 1.48×10^{-1} 29. $\frac{9}{16}$ 30. $\frac{256}{a^8}$ 31. $\frac{81}{x^{12}}$ 32. $\frac{125}{27}$

33. $\frac{81}{16}$ 34. $\frac{a^{12}}{b^3}$ 35. $\frac{x^3}{y^2}$ 36. $\frac{a^8b^4}{c^{12}}$ 37. $\frac{4x^6y^4}{z^2}$

38. $\frac{27b^9c^{12}}{a^6}$ 39. $\frac{1}{x^8z^6}$ 40. 1 41. $\frac{64m^4p^8}{n^4}$ 42. $\frac{b^{12}}{a^6}$

43. 1 44. $\frac{p^3r^4}{q^4}$

Practice 8-8: Mixed Exercises

1. c^6 2. $\frac{y^8z^{20}}{x^{12}}$ 3. $\frac{y^8z^{20}}{x^{12}}$ 4. $\frac{a^{10}}{b^{15}}$ 5. 3^3 6. $\frac{a^{12}}{b^8}$ 7. $\frac{9}{4}$

8. $\frac{q^4}{p^{12}r^{20}}$ 9. $\frac{a^8}{b^{12}}$ 10. 7^3 11. a^2b^5 12. $\frac{a^{10}}{b^{30}}$ 13. $\frac{64}{9}$

14. z^{10} 15. $25b^8c^6$ 16. $\frac{x^5z^8}{y^{14}}$ 17. $\frac{1}{m^4}$ 18. 1 19. $\frac{s^8}{t^2}$

20. $\frac{32a^{15}}{b^{10}c^{15}}$ 21. $\frac{x^8}{y^2z^8}$ 22. $\frac{1}{h^5}$ 23. $\frac{1}{4^2}$ 24. $\frac{1}{3^3}$

25. $\frac{x^3}{y^6}$ 26. $\frac{n^{24}}{m^{12}}$ 27. $\frac{1}{4^3}$ 28. $\frac{b^{30}}{a^{15}}$ 29. $\frac{1}{n^6}$ 30. $\frac{s^7}{r}$

31. $\frac{1}{n^{12}}$ 32. $\frac{1}{m^2n^2}$ 33. 5.75×10^{-5} 34. 2.52×10^2

35. 2.07×10^4 36. 2×10^4 37. 1.9×10^{-3}

38. 8×10^1 39. 6.08×10^3 40. 2×10^{-11}

41. 4×10^8 42. 1.72×10^9 43. 3.33×10^{-3}

44. 7×10^8 45. 3.68×10^2 46. 3×10^{-5}

47. 7×10^1 48. 4.06×10^{-2}

✔ Checkpoint 1: For use after 8-3

1. $y = 16{,}000 \times 0.84^x$; $4721.44

2. $f(x) = 5000 \times 3^x$; $405,000

3. $y = 175{,}000 \times 1.025^x$; 235,356

4a. $y = 29 \times 1.324^x$ **4b.** 6000

5. exponential decay,

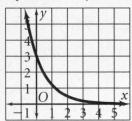

6. exponential growth,

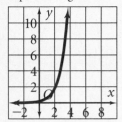

7. exponential growth,

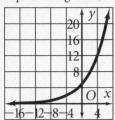

✔ Checkpoint 2: For use after 8-6

1. 1 **2.** 9 **3.** -64 **4.** $\frac{4}{3}$ **5.** -125 **6.** $-\frac{9}{4}$ **7.** none

8. 4.8×10^9 **9.** 3.5×10^4 **10.** 2.4×10^3 **11.** 3×10^{-11}

12a. 1.496×10^8; 2.279×10^8 **12b.** 7.83×10^7 km

Chapter Assessment, Form A

1. $\frac{4}{7}$, 28, 196 **2.** $\frac{1}{9}$, 4, 24 **3.** 10, 16.9, 21.97 **4.** $\frac{15}{4}$, $\frac{12}{5}$, $\frac{48}{25}$

5a. $16,000; $64,000 **5b.** $y = 2000 \cdot 2^x$

6a. 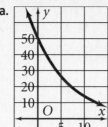 **6b.** 5.4 yr

7. Answers may vary. Sample: $2500 at 4% for 3 years. Compounded annually: $y = 2500 \cdot 1.04^x$; $2812.16 after 3 yr. Compounded quarterly: $y = 2500 \cdot 1.01^x$; $2817.06 after 3 years. **8.** No. Although y gets close to 0 as x gets larger, $y > 0$ for all values of x. **9.** B

10.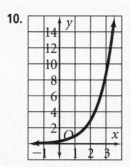

11.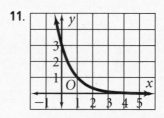

12.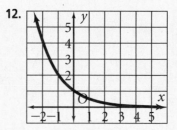

13. $x < 0$; $y > 0$ for all x. **14.** 5.98×10^{13} Btu

15. 1.4×10^8 m **16.** 4.8×10^4 **17.** 1.19×10^{-1}

18. -7×10^{11} **19.** 8×10^1 **20.** $\frac{a^4}{b^7}$ **21.** $\frac{1}{0.93^2}$

22. $\frac{p^3 r^6}{q^3}$ **23.** $\frac{n^{15}}{m^6}$ **24.** $\frac{y^7}{x^7}$ **25.** $-\frac{u^4}{v^2}$

26a. $y = 1000 \cdot 1.004^{12x}$ **26b.** $1049.07; $1100.55

27a. decay **27b.** 16.29 min **27c.** 8.8 min

Chapter 8 Answers (continued)

Chapter Assessment, Form B

1. $\frac{1}{8}$, 8, 128 **2.** $\frac{3}{256}$, 6, 384 **3.** 64, 8, 2 **4.** $\frac{9}{4}$, $\frac{16}{3}$, $\frac{256}{27}$

5a. 3375; 30,375 **5b.** $y = 125 \cdot 3^x$.

6a. 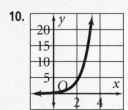 **6b.** 2.3 days

7. Answers may vary. Sample: a quantity that starts at 1500 and decreases 5%/yr for x yr **8.** If the exponent is positive, the number is greater than 1. If the exponent is negative, the number is less than 1. **9.** D

10.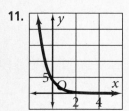

11.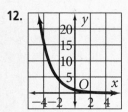

12.

13. Samantha's work is correct. By definition, $4^{-3} = \frac{1}{4^3}$

14. 7.5×10^1 **15.** 2.69×10^2 **16.** 6.1×10^{-7}

17. 4.4×10^6 **18.** 3.2×10^{10} **19.** 3.4×10^1 **20.** $\frac{x^3 z^4}{y^3}$

21. $\frac{s}{r^5}$ **22.** $2a$ **23.** -7.1^2 **24.** $\frac{2m^2}{n^4}$ **25.** $\frac{3j^6}{2l^3}$

26a. $y = 500 \cdot 1.016^x$ **26b.** $567.70; 686.82

27a. decay; 4% **27b.** Answers may vary. Sample: In 1988, the population was 52,645. **27c.** Answers may vary. Sample: In 2008, the population will be 11,160.

Alternative Assessment

TASK 1 Scoring Guide:

3 Student writes, solves, and graphs problems that clearly demonstrate an in-depth understanding of the mathematical principles involved.

2 Student shows a solid understanding of the mathematical principles.

1 Student shows a limited understanding of the mathematical principles involved.

0 Response is missing or inappropriate.

TASK 2 Scoring Guide:

3 Student selects appropriate values for the variable and solves all parts of the problem with no mistakes.

2 Student selects appropriate values for the variable and solves all parts of the problem with only minor mistakes.

1 Student either selects inappropriate values for the variable or has significant computational errors.

0 Response is missing or inappropriate.

TASK 3 Scoring Guide:

3 Student presents an explanation that thoroughly discusses the appropriate time to use scientific notation. Problem has sufficient detail to augment discussion.

2 Student's explanation shows a good degree of understanding of scientific notation. Problem could be more clear or have more detail.

1 Student's explanation does not make a clear argument for when or how to use scientific notation.

0 Response is missing or inappropriate.

TASK 4 Scoring Guide:

a. $\frac{2b^3}{a^4}$ **b.** $\frac{1}{y^5}$ **c.** $\frac{4}{-3k^3n^5}$ **d.** $6x^7y^3$ **e.** $54x^{10}$

3 Student identifies and corrects all errors.

2 Student identifies and corrects most errors.

1 Student identifies and corrects some of the errors.

0 Response is missing or inappropriate.

Chapter 8 Answers (continued)

Cumulative Review

1. C **2.** A **3.** D **4.** B **5.** C **6.** B **7.** A **8.** D **9.** B **10.** C

11. B **12.** A **13.** C **14.** B

15. vertex: $\left(\frac{5}{2}, -\frac{9}{4}\right)$; x-intercepts are at 1 and 4.

16. Answers will vary. Sample: You deposit $250 in an account which pays 5% interest compounded quarterly. How much will you have in the account after 6 yr? $336.84

17.

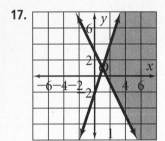

Standardized Test Practice

1. A **2.** C **3.** D **4.** A **5.** D **6.** A **7.** E **8.** B **9.** C **10.** C

11. A **12.** $y = 7.5 \cdot 1.05^x$ **13.** Answers may vary.

14. 1×10^{10} **15.** $\dfrac{a^{16}c^5}{b}$ **16.** $\dfrac{c^5 d^4 f^3}{a^2 b^2}$ **17.** -1

18. 6250 **19.** 48,000